Edited extracts

from oral history recordings and written memories

given by the people of Market Bos' ' District

for

Compiled and edited
by
Glynis Oakley
Joan Tomlinson
Ingrid Davison
Beth Dawes
Eric Colley

Initial layout by Bernard Boyce

LOTTERY FUNDED

Printed by Paradigm Print UK Ltd Leicester

These memories, either oral or written, are all personal recollections and, as such, no attempt has been made to check details. The publisher can neither accept liability for any errors nor for the stated opinions from third parties.

These recollections mainly cover a sixty year period from 1920s to 1980s, with the last chapter from Congerstone Primary School bringing us up to the present. The original interviews are kept at the East Midlands Oral History Archive at the Record Office, Wigston. www.le.ac.uk/emoha. Please contact them for further details. A CD is available giving a shortened version of the audio recordings and can be purchased separately.

Additional editorial notes are in italics.

ACKNOWLEDGEMENTS

We would like to thank the following people who so kindly allowed the Market Bosworth Society to interview them over the last few years and for those who allowed us to use their written memories:
Susan Andrews (née Glyde), Barbara Arm (née Trivett), George Armson, Brenda Bates (née Loseby), Dennis Bream, Ray Carter, George and Pat Cooling (née Salmon), Derek and Joy Crane (née Greenfield), Laura Croman (née Hicklin), Ingrid Davison (née Cheshire), Alan Eames, Gordon and Jill Earp (née Kirkman), John Ensor, David Fitt, Harry Frost, Patrick Green, Maurice Harris, Olive Hicklin (née Neville), Angela Hutton, Robert Jarvis, Philip Jenkins, Jim Lampard, Robert Leake, Peter and Sheila Loseby (née Gamble), Colin Lowe in an extract from 'Down your Way' 1976, Diana Morgan, Brian Oakley, Paul Oakley, Kay Palmer (née Quincey), Roger Payne, Fred Proudman, Arthur Rowlinson, David Salmon, Martin Shepherd Cyril Smith, Winifred Smith (née Pratt), Reg and Nancy Sperry (née Redfern), Blanche Symonds (née Johnson), Robert Taylor, John Thorp, Mary Vernon, Marjorie Vero (née Neville), Alwyn Whitney and the pupils and teachers from Congerstone Primary School.

We would also like to thank the following members of the Market Bosworth Society who helped in the compilation of this book: Jonathon Green, Tony and Anne Howlett, Fiona Helliwell, Barbara Tristram, Robert and Pauline Leake, Peter Ellis and Brian Wilson.

Thanks also to the interviewers: Sue Naylor, Sue Andrews, Ingrid Davison, Peter Ellis, Audrey Boston, Tony Howlett, Glynis Oakley and especially to Eric Colley who also most ably transferred the information to disc. The interviews have been transcribed most proficiently by Michelle McLean, Leila Novell and Sue Andrews.

The proof readers were: Beryl Baker, Joan Tomlinson, Beth Dawes and T B Heathcote.

Our thanks also go to Ivan Ould, former Chairman of the Society, for writing the Foreword and to Chris Peat, for writing the Introduction.

Many thanks to John Oakley for the design and layout of the front and back covers; to Alan Spencer for allowing us to use his drawings of the forge and the archway in front of the Water Tower, Bosworth Hall; to Eric Colley, Edward Smith, Walter Baynes and numerous others who kindly lent us their photographs; to Paul Macmillan, English teacher at the Dixie Grammar School. Finally for the support and encouragement received from the present members of the Market Bosworth Society, namely: Alan Weston, Susan Andrews, Angela Hutton, Len Staniland and Peter Loseby.

We hope that you, the reader, enjoy these recollections from the people of Market Bosworth and the surrounding villages.

CONTENTS

'We all fall down'

Children playing in the road outside the school at Carlton

FOREWORD

Memories are made from real life experiences, and unless recorded, are passed on from one generation to the next by word of mouth. The Market Bosworth Society has always targeted the recording of memories as a major part of its heritage work. This book is an excellent example of the use of the memories of local residents, giving a vibrant insight into life in and around Market Bosworth within living memory.

I was lucky enough to be born at a time when health and safety did not rule our lives, when children could play away from home without being preyed upon, when rationing of food was commonplace but love within the family was boundless. Can you remember an age when a family did not have anything other than a radio, where the electricity and gas stopped unless money was put in the meter, where hot water had to be boiled in a kettle, you bathed in a tin bath, and the toilet was down the yard?

Read on and enjoy a super book about our local heritage. Play and Childhood Memories, Hearth and Home, the Bosworth Show, Fair and Cattle Market, and many, many more memories are recorded here for your interest and enjoyment.

Our thanks go to those local people who were prepared to have their memories recorded, and to those willing volunteers who interviewed, recorded and transcribed those memories thus enabling the compilation of this book.

Ivan Ould
County Councillor for the Market Bosworth Division of Leicestershire County Council for thirteen years.

The Arms of the Market Bosworth Rural District Council

INTRODUCTION

This volume contains personal recollections of life in Market Bosworth from about 1920 to the present day. It is intended to be a record of commonplace activities and local events; the routines and details of daily life which make a community, and which lie behind the greater developments recorded in history books. The material has been extracted from interviews given by local people, many of whom have lived in the area for all of their lives. It is important to remember that these are all personal recollections and often give only one side of a story. No attempt has been made to check names, dates, times or places, and the information given may not be totally factually correct.

It is common to view the past through rose-tinted glasses, but there can be no doubt that material living conditions have been transformed since the Second World War, let alone 1920. The minutes of Market Bosworth Parish Council show evidence of change, being hand-written from the day of the first meeting on 4th December 1894 until the end of 1973, then typed, and now word-processed. The black ink writing of 1894 is as legible today as when it was put on the page; will the same be true of today's printer inks in 120 years time?

There have been many changes in local government since 1920. The last Parish Overseers were appointed in 1926, and the last Parish Constables in 1929. The Parish handcuffs were returned by the Police in 1930 and presented to the Parish Clerk. The most far-reaching change occurred in 1974, when Market Bosworth Rural District Council was merged with Hinckley Urban District Council to create Hinckley & Bosworth Borough Council. This proposal was bitterly opposed at the time, as it was clear that it would mean that rural affairs would be controlled by an urban majority. So it has proved, and out of the 34 Borough Councillors today, only 13 represent rural areas.

The provision of street lighting has always been an important function of the Parish Council. Before 1926, Market Bosworth was lit by gaslight, and the lamplighter would walk round at sunset to light the lamps. The Rural District Council took over fire fighting duties in 1939, when the telephone number for the fire brigade was Bosworth 222. Today we have a retained service. In the 1930s there were discussions about a sewerage scheme for the town at an estimated cost of £4,000, and this is when the first sewage works near the railway sidings off Station Road was developed. This works was enlarged in 1962 and new sewer pipes laid all through the town, causing great disruption in 1965. In 1992 this system was replaced by a completely new sewerage works near Carlton.

The Parish Council Minutes for the war years are generally brief and not very informative, given the number of military dumps, stores, depots and camps - for both allied troops and prisoners of war - in the area. In 1943 it was reported that the parish had raised £15,794-12s-1d for Wings for Victory Week. VE Day in 1945 was celebrated with a tea and concert for all Market Bosworth children, organised by Mrs Hutchinson, Mrs Loseby and other ladies. Mr Hills' loud speaker equipment was engaged to provide music for dancing. A similar event was held later in the year for VJ Day.

Post-war housing was discussed at several meetings in 1943-44, with the Parish Council taking the view that Bosworth people in the forces would want and expect houses to live in when they returned home, and that at least thirty houses were needed rather than the ten allocated. This debate rumbled on for some years, but led to the construction of Bosworth's first council houses in Beckett Avenue, named after Mr Edgar Beckett who helped bring the project to fruition.

In 1953 there were many complaints about the annual Mayfair in the Market Place, leading to a very long and strongly worded resolution from the Parish Council. This led to an agreement with the Showmen's Guild that in 1954 the Fair would be limited to Friday, Saturday and Monday, the loud speakers would be turned down, and the pitches would be rearranged so as not to cause obstruction. This seems to have worked, as no further complaints were recorded.

In the 1960s, Sir Wolstan Dixie submitted two planning applications to develop Bosworth Park. The first scheme comprised 40 acres of housing with a park of 35 acres; the second proposed 860 houses and 6 shops. The plans were refused, but a very much smaller proposal was approved and led to the construction of Cedar Drive and Chestnut Close in 1970. In 1966 an application was made for a Club Licence for Bosworth Park House, which later became the Inn on the Park, and was eventually demolished to make way for Sycamore Way in 1995. In 1970 the land comprising the current Country Park was acquired by Leicestershire County Council in a far sighted move which ensured the preservation of the historic parkland setting of the eastern side of the town.

Developments up until about 1980 have been succinctly reviewed by Peter Foss. Since that time, the site of the former Council depot off Back Lane has become Moorland Close (1988), the Cattle Market has closed down and become Market Mews (1996), and the Timber & Fireproofing factory has become Pipistrelle Drive (2005). On the recreational front, Bosworth Water Trust has been created on wet farmland off Coton Lane (1988), school playing fields have been created (1990) and a pavilion built (2009) off Barton Road, a golf course has been built around the north western side of the town (opening 2010), and a small camping and caravan site has been developed off Cadeby Lane (2004).

At first sight, the countryside setting of Market Bosworth does not appear to have changed much over the past ninety years. It was fortunate that the Bosworth Estate was bought by a small number of landowners who have pursued relatively conservative land management policies. All the same, the felling of woods and ploughing of meadow land during the war marked the start of a decline in wildlife. Since then many hedgerows have been lost, roadside gardens have been abandoned, large tracts of land have been drained and farming practices have led to further losses. The persistence of mixed farming, the underlying geology, innate conservatism and local support for country sports of all kinds have been instrumental in conserving the local landscape. However, some small parcels of land have been sold, and hobby farms, wildlife sites and stables have begun to spring up around the town. The town itself has expanded and playing fields and a golf course have been developed around it but, the overall pattern of the Bosworth Estate remains and open countryside is still only five minutes walk away from the Market Place.

The town centre retains much of its character thanks to the nucleation of the town around the Market Place, with development to the east limited by St Peter's Church, Bosworth Hall and Market Bosworth Country Park. It now enjoys statutory protection through the designation of the Market Bosworth Conservation Area in 1974 and its extension in 1996. A Town Trail was published by the Market Bosworth Society in 2009 and is currently available from outlets in the town centre.

Chris Peat

Sources
Foss, P, 1983. The History of Market Bosworth. Sycamore Press, Wymondham. ISBN 0-905837-19-3.

Market Bosworth Parish Council Minutes 1894-1950. Leicestershire Record Office DE7279.

Market Bosworth Parish Council Minutes 1950-1967, and 1967-1976. Leicestershire Record Office DE5849.

Drawing of the archway leading into the former glasshouses in the walled garden, Bosworth Hall by A G Spencer

CHILDHOOD MEMORIES

WHAT OPPORTUNITIES DID RURAL MARKET BOSWORTH OFFER FOR PLAY AND ADVENTURE? THESE MEMORIES SEEM TO EXEMPLIFY A TIME OF FUN AND FREEDOM.

Contributors to this section were Olive Hicklin, Ingrid Davison, Laura Croman, Jill Earp, Barbara Arm, Cyril Smith, George Armson, John Thorp, Pat Cooling, Peter Loseby, Blanche Symonds, Angela Hutton and Joy Crane.

George Armson writes: Lots of us would make a maypole and go and sing at people's doors. The money they gave us was saved for the Mayfair on May 8th. Our early days were spent roaming and picking blackberries. Mr Chimes would always give some money for the mushrooms we collected. When it was hot, as it used to be for the holidays, we would dam the Stoney Brook down in Hollier's fields. We would then use that as a swimming pool and play all sorts of sports. When winter came, what a happy but cold place to be, was Silk Hill.

Various rhymes, games and places to play were often influenced by the season or month of the year, such as this one as remembered by Barbara Arm:

O maypole day is a very fine day
Please remember the maypole.
Around the maypole we can trot
See what a maypole we have got.

Dressed in ribbons and tied in bows
See what a maypole we can show.
With a jig and a jag and a merry fine flag
Please remember the maypole.

Let your money be great or small
We've got a purse that will hold it all.
If you haven't got a penny a ha'penny will do
If you haven't got a ha'penny, God bless you.

Barbara Arm writes: On May Day a doll was put on a tray and surrounded by flowers, marigolds and lady's smock, and ribbons et cetera. This was covered with a veil or piece of white netting. If the children received a penny, the doll was shown by lifting the piece of net. I attended weekly dance classes in the Parish Hall with about a dozen other children. These were run by Miss Bowers, the daughter of Canon Bowers. The piano was played by Mrs Gibbs who also taught at the Infant School.

Maypole dancing in the Market Place

'SPRIG OF OAK LEAVES IN YOUR LAPEL'

I remember children singing:

Sutton for mutton　　　　　　　*Higham on the Hill*
Bosworth for beef　　　　　　　*Stoke in the dale*
Shenton for pretty girls　　　　　*Wykin for buttermilk*
Carlton for thieves　　　　　　　*Hinckley for ale.*

Cyril Smith writes: **On May Day Mrs Booton would make a maypole. This was hoops fastened to the top of a pole and decorated with flowers and ribbons. Someone would carry the maypole and we would walk behind, holding long ribbons attached to the hoop. We would parade all round the village singing a song, something like this:**

> *Maypole day, maypole day*
> *If you don't give us a holiday*
> *We'll all run away.*

The village commemorated Royal Oak Day. On this day if you hadn't a sprig of oak leaves in your lapel, all the other kids who would be carrying stinging nettles, would sting your legs.

Ingrid Davison – There was a favourite willow, namely, Hollow Tree House, which grew in the corner of a field close to Silk Hill. We would go in there in the summer, climb into it and sit in it. It was a den. You wouldn't let other children in if you were there first!

Winter was really good because my dad, being a carpenter, made a sledge with metal runners. We would go sledging on Silk Hill. He also made kites and used waxy, bread paper to cover the wooden frame. We would take a kite to Silk Hill on windy days.

My dad constructed two different layouts for train sets for my brothers. One train set was Hornby OO and the other was Triang. The Duchess of Montrose was the name of one of the Hornby trains. In addition my dad made me a big dolls' house, complete with lights and stairs.

Painting of Silk Hill by Kate E Thorpe

'BOY DID WE RUN, STRAIGHT THROUGH THE BROOK'

Olive Hicklin – Me and my friends would hide from Mr Robinson, the water bailiff, who lived between Congerstone and Bilstone. There were loads of willow trees hanging over the water and we would climb them. When he found us he would shout, 'Come out of that tree!' We loved playing in the trees over the water. It was really dangerous because none of us could swim and the river was fast in some places.

Cyril Smith writes: Most of the villagers at Norton juxta Twycross had their milk from the local farms. One afternoon I was sent with a friend to fetch milk from George Henton's farm. We decided not to go all the way round by road but to take a short cut across a very large field which had a fast flowing brook through the middle of it. When we had almost reached the brook, we noticed in the corner of the field what we thought was a cow; until we saw it start to charge towards us. We then realised it was a bull! Boy, did we run; straight through the brook and up the field on the other side, just getting over the gate opposite the farm as the bull came charging up. Needless to say, we went back down the road!

Making a catapult was a time consuming occupation. We would spend hours searching for the right piece of forked wood to make it. We made the rubbers from old tyre inner tubes and the sling from a tongue of an old pair of boots. We would put a tin on a fence or wall and take pot shots at it. We were all pretty good with the old 'catty'.

Blanche Symonds writes: The Market Place was the playground for where she skipped and played ball games with her friends. Along with other children she would walk down Sutton Lane and open the gate for passing traffic, sometimes getting a penny or sixpence as a reward. Or they would take a picnic down Barton Road to Stoney Brook where they paddled and fished for tiddlers. At other times she went fruit picking. She remembers going to the slaughterhouse and seeing the animals being killed. The pig's bladder would be blown up and often served as a ball for their games.

INEVITABLY, THERE WERE THE OCCASIONAL ACCIDENTS

Laura Croman – We used to play games on the chapel wall opposite to where I lived. One day my ball shot into the road and I shot after it, only to be knocked down by a cyclist. He came from Ibstock and his wife sent him back the next day to present me with half-a-crown which paid for the family dinner so I didn't see much of it! I had a cut knee which of course got gravel in it, so I had to put up with mother's administrations which included lint dipped in boiling hot water, which she removed with some scissors cos it was too hot for her to touch - but it wasn't too hot to put on my injured knee!

The War Memorial

'WE HAD TO USE A SAUCEPAN TO BAIL OUT THE WATER'

Jill Earp – We played a variety of games such as snobs or five stones, rounders and marbles in the playground, skipping, whip and top, hoopla, hopscotch and ball games. I had my first bike at about eleven years old, the bike was second hand.

Barbara Arm writes: Sir Thomas Cope lived at Osbaston Hall and every year we had a party there. In the spinney opposite to the Hall was an ice house, where meat and game were kept fresh. In the Hall field were two big ponds, one a fish pond and the other a boating lake. The Copes had a house at Folkestone where they usually spent the summer. Somehow we children knew when they were away and we would get a boat from the boathouse and row across to the island in the middle of the lake. The boat had a small leak so we had to use a saucepan to bail out the water.

George Armson writes: When I was young we used to come and work the bellows for Mr Wothers and Mr Chimes (*at the forge*) then they allowed us to go and get some apples from the orchard next door.

When at the Junior School, Mr Cooper had a little shop opposite where we used to go and get some sweets and he would show us how to play the big drum. The boxers came to the Dixie Arms, one being Larry Gains who came out for a walk on the Sunday afternoon. Larry spoke to most people and my brother, Fred, said, 'Hello Larry'. Whenever he saw us he would pick up Fred, give him some money, then get us all together and throw money to us. Most mornings all the boxers used to go for a run around Cadeby and back via the Bull in the Oak.

Angela Hutton – We played a lot of indoor and outdoor games, even in the winter time. Several of us would meet up near to the Council Offices to play. Indoors we liked to play Monopoly. My brother, David, had a set of Mecanno, which we would sometimes help to construct. One outdoor game we played (Fox and Hounds) we nicknamed 'arrows'. This was where someone would go on ahead and leave a trail of chalked arrows and the remainder followed the trail until this person was found. We also played a lot of two and three ball games with tennis balls, which were thrown at the wall both underarm and overarm, in juggling style, and we would say rhymes as we were throwing the balls. There was a large tree that we used to play on down Station Road, near to Godsons Hill, that we called the swinging tree. The tree had a large branch that we would climb on and sit with our legs dangling each side of the branch and then perform a seesaw action to make the branch move up and down.

Boxer Larry Gains with Mr and Mrs Granger

'THE HORSE WOULD TURN ITS HEAD ROUND AND NOD TO CLEM'

Peter Loseby – I would often stop by the forge on my way home from the Junior School to watch Clem, the blacksmith, shoe a horse. Clem in his brown leather apron would nestle the horse's hoof between his knees and swiftly remove the old shoe, take a paring knife out of his pocket on his leather apron and remove the excess hoof before placing the hot new shoe on the hoof which created a cloud of smoke. The acrid smell of the smoke would make you gasp but not Clem, he just simply ignored it. Clem worked swiftly and quietly. Rarely did I see the horse get skittish but just stood there allowing him to manoeuvre each foot into the required position. I swear that very often the horse would stamp its foot down as though checking it was a good job done then turn its head round and nod to Clem!

The forge, a drawing by A G Spencer

John Thorp – When we lived in Park Street, Clem who was the blacksmith was a bit deaf and his wife used to shout a lot. You could hear her shouting right down the road. We used to knock at the door and run and she used to come out shouting at us - we used to get up to a few tricks! I think he wasn't as deaf as he pretended to be sometimes.

'DAD HAD TO TAKE HER COAT OFF AND WRING THE WATER OUT OF IT'

Pre-school I had scarlet fever and I went into Sunnyside, at Hinckley, because I think that was an illness which required isolation. I went to live on my uncle's farm, Culloden Farm near Twycross, for a year or so. I enjoyed that. I remember, even now, what animals were kept in each shed.

Uncle George was a heavy horse man and I just remember my grandfather who lived there, he was one-time champion sheepdog man, Champion of England. I still have one or two of his cups. I have recollections of him trialling sheep.

One memory I have got is going on the train from Bosworth Station on excursions to Skegness and Matlock Bath. I was probably one of the last people to go.

After school I used to make a bit of money by selling wood, chopping the cases up from the fruit and vegetables and selling it as firewood round the village from a truck. I also had a few Banties which I used to keep at my grandmother's and I used to do a lot of gardening for her as well, as she was a widow.

Olive Hicklin – While Mum was in hospital my sister had to go back and serve her notice at Prestwold Hall for a month, so I was left on my own. One Sunday, when Dad had gone to see Mum, there was a dreadful storm. It was a cloudburst; I had got the dinner on the stove. We had to brush the water through the house because it came down the lane and through the front door. I have never seen anything like it. It also dislodged soot as it came down the chimney and knocked the saucepan lids off. I got soot in the potatoes and I had to start all over again. Oh dear, it was one of the most dreadful Sundays I have ever had in my life.

Madge, my sister, had gone with my dad and they were on their bikes and she was wearing this lovely coat. They went the Bagworth way and came back through Barlestone and Thornton and they were coming along the top road when Dad said, 'Come on, hurry up. If we hurry up we will miss this storm!' He had to push her into the hedge because it came down like a sheet. When she came out she couldn't move, as her coat was that heavy and wet. Dad had to take her coat off and wring the water out of it. Of course, when they got home there was all the mess caused by the rain and soot.

'I SAW THE ANGELS COMING FOR ME'

Cyril Smith writes: Ozzie Lees, from Norton juxta Twycross, had a flat top coal lorry and he made a box top which he bolted onto it. He had a couple of wooden forms inside with steps at the back. One of the highlights of the year was when he used to take us to Market Bosworth Flower Show. I remember coming home when a drunk, I can't remember who, always stood on the steps. We would get over the humpbacked bridges at Carlton and the one before Congerstone but he always fell off at the one on the road to Bilstone.

Where I lived there was one wash house shared between, I believe, four families. Everyone had their own wash-day. At Christmas time everyone made their Christmas puddings. They were always in a white basin with a piece of sheeting tied and knotted over the top. Everybody put an identification mark on the puddings, then one day the fire was lit under the copper and all the puddings were boiled together. It saved coal doing it like that.

Pat Cooling – At Sedgemere we had an absolutely idyllic life, it was freedom. My brother used to have his friends down there and go swimming. Mother used to get the tea, take it down to the summerhouse, just sandwiches and cups of tea, and we used to play tennis and Dad used to play bowls. She wouldn't have us getting bored.

The year that they sold Sedgemere, there used to be dances at St Peter's Hall. After the dance we used to go back down to Sedgemere to go swimming at midnight. The game we played was to get into the boat, take it to the middle, rock it and let it fill with water. We would then get off it and people swam back. One particular fellow got in it and he couldn't swim but they got him out. All I can remember him saying in the kitchen was, 'Mr Salmon, I saw the angels coming for me'.

Joy Crane – Mum would go to Nuneaton on a Saturday morning on the bus, because she didn't drive at the time, and she would do the extra bits of shopping. She always came back laden. She used to have to walk up the hill because the bus didn't bring you up through Wellsborough, but dropped you off at the bottom of the hill. I do know that I went to meet her several times. As I got older, about ten or eleven years of age, I was the one who had to go to Nuneaton to collect the cash and the men would be waiting for their wages when I got home. I was terrified that someone was going to pinch the cash so I did all sorts of things to hide it. I've often thought about it because I don't think the banks would let a child have the money these days but I think we knew the bank manager well, so I suppose they made some arrangement that we did it.

Sedgemere, Station Road

HEARTH AND HOME

LIFE IN THE HOME WAS VERY DIFFERENT IN THE EARLY 20TH CENTURY. GAS AND ELECTRICITY WERE NOT AVAILABLE TO THE MAJORITY OF HOMES. THERE WAS ALSO NO MAINS WATER, HOT OR COLD AND MOST HAD NO CONNECTION TO THE SEWERS. RADIO WAS IN THE EARLY STAGES OF DEVELOPMENT AND TELEVISION ONLY BECAME WIDESPREAD WITH THE CORONATION OF QUEEN ELIZABETH II IN 1953.

Contributors to this section were Barbara Arm, Blanche Symonds, Laura Croman, Jim Lampard, Olive Hicklin, David Salmon, Gordon Earp, Angela Hutton and Kay Palmer.

Barbara Arm writes: When I was young there was no electricity; I think that came in 1931 or '32. We had oil lamps hanging from the ceiling, these were brass lamps which had to be trimmed and filled daily with oil. It was wonderful when the Aladdin lamp came. It had a very delicate white mantel and gave a much brighter light, but this was only to be used in the dining room.

Our first wireless was a 'cat's whisker' type and had two headphones. However, we children were not allowed to use them.

When Mother first went to Osbaston, she employed two maids but one left. As you can imagine help was needed with five girls and one boy. There was a very big black grate in the kitchen which had ovens on either side of the fire and one long oven over the whole length of the fire on top. This had to be lit every morning and be

cleaned. A fire was also put into the dining room. Every Friday morning the dining room carpet was cleaned by putting old tea leaves on to it and then brushed up with a hard brush. I suppose this was to prevent the dust getting around. Every Monday a woman was fetched from Market Bosworth to do the week's washing.

We had breakfast in the kitchen on Sundays in winter, and then were dressed in our best dresses for the day. Until after dinner, which was always in the dining room, we wore white linen pinafores which always had beautifully embroidered lace tops to keep our dresses clean. In the afternoon we were allowed to go for a walk whilst our parents rested.

Above: Aladdin lamp
Right: Diagram of a typical cat's whisker radio

'SHE REMEMBERS HAMS HANGING IN THE KITCHEN'

At Osbaston Hall there was a big lake with an island and we would get the boat from the boathouse and row to the island, we being my sister, brother and myself.

Water was carried to most houses from the village pumps. Saturday night was bath night and in the winter, whilst we were young, it took place in the kitchen. The copper in the scullery was filled with water and boiled and an enormous bath, shaped like a huge tin saucer, was carried into the kitchen. When we were older we used the bathroom but all the hot water had to be carried upstairs.

The carpets from a lot of the houses in Bosworth were taken up into the Park. The men would take the carpet corners and shake it and then turn it over and drag it up and down the Park to clean it. This was always done at spring-cleaning time.

Blanche Symonds writes: She was one of eight children, born in 1934, and has lived at Richmond House, Market Place, since she was six weeks old, and she recalls her early childhood when her dad kept pigs down the Back Lane. She also remembers hams hanging in the kitchen. Her father had an allotment on Harry Weston's field, now Weston Drive, where he grew all the family's vegetables. They were almost self-sufficient.

Life was very happy but with large families times were sometimes difficult. There was no hot water at Richmond House until 1957 and although there was a toilet in the bathroom, flushing was done with a bucket of water.

Top right: Osbaston Hall lake
Left: Richmond House, Market Place

'FOR WATER YOU HAD TO WALK DOWN THE HILL AND UP A YARD TO A PUMP AT THE TOP'

Water for the whole house was heated on the kitchen range. Once a week the tin bath would be brought into the kitchen and filled for the family bath time. A pump in the back kitchen provided water from a well. The coal fire in the range had bricks stacked at the back to conserve coal and these were only removed to provide a more effective fire for baking day. All the cooking was done on this range which gave heat to the kitchen but the rest of the rooms had paraffin heaters or no heat at all.

Laura Croman — My family home was in the terrace that once stood opposite the chapel in Barton Road. There was a small living room at the front where we had our meals, not all together as it was not large enough. At the back was a large room but the floor was always damp and there was only a tiny little window which looked out onto the yard and the privies, and a small sink but we had quite a happy childhood. The stairs were full of woodworm and you could see through into the room below. My brothers had a very small bedroom which went off the stairs but it was very dark. My mother's and father's bedroom was quite big. My sister and I had the attic upstairs.

There was no water laid on so you had to walk down the hill, right to the bottom and up a yard to a pump at the top. That's where the drying ground was for wash-day, you had a regular day, ours was Thursday, if it rained on that day it was just too bad. My mother did the washing indoors on a backless chair with a big bath. Father fetched two buckets of water, and before we went to school, we children had to fetch the rest, starting with a full bucket, with half of it landing in your shoes on the way up the hill.

Granny Stevens lived next door to Long's slaughter house at the bottom, and she was the only person allowed by the Squire, Mr Delius, to collect sticks from underneath his trees. She had a black apron and she used to fill it with sticks every day; we children used to go and help her.

Terraced houses, Barton Road

'A HORSE DRAWN CART, KNOWN AS THE MARMALADE PAN, CAME ROUND WEEKLY TO EMPTY THE TOILETS'

The toilets were up a backyard so you had to go out of the door and down past one house and up a long entry which had a bend in it, and at night it was terrifying to me because the boys used to hide there and jump out at you. There were about six toilets, I suppose, each one allotted to a certain house. The toilets were emptied once a week. A horse-drawn cart came round to empty them and was known as the 'marmalade pan'.

Later when the family moved to The Crescent in 1931, when I was eleven years old, wonders on wonders, we had tap water, not hot but cold tap water, and the toilet was only just two steps from the back door, a great improvement. There was a garden at the back and front. My dad grew potatoes on the front the first year but he got told off as that was for flowers only. My dad had an allotment, as well as the back garden, which was on Harry Weston's field where Weston Drive is now.

My mother would undo woollies, time and time again and knit them up again and so, being younger, I used to finish up with short sleeves. I valued them because they were knitted by my mum for me. The doctor's wife, Mrs Keeling, distributed things to the poor. In those days, when a child was absent from school, the excuse was often, 'He's had to stay in bed, Miss, his shoes have gone to be mended', and of course, we all wore pass-me-down clothes, which were not very elegant. Mrs Keeling distributed things from the Hall so I often got things from one of the Hall children; I always remember a lovely coat I got from there.

Angela Hutton – We lived in a terraced house, four in a row, and it had an outside toilet and a coal house adjacent to this. There was a copper in the corner of the kitchen that heated the water. When I was really young we used to take turns to bathe in a tin bath in the kitchen. We had a hand pump situated on the kitchen sink and a well in the garden. The pump had a large handle which was pumped up and down to draw the water.

'WE WOULD SIT ROUND THE FIRE AND SING'

JIM LAMPARD WAS ASKED:
HOW DID PEOPLE KEEP THEIR
MEAT?

Jim Lampard (butcher) – I don't know, but there was a lady at Upton, Mrs Treadwell, and when they took the meat round on Friday afternoon, she always had a hole ready in the garden where she would bury a biscuit tin with her meat in.

Olive Hicklin – There were nine of us. I've got four brothers and there were five girls. I'm the second eldest. I would like to tell you how we spent our nights. We would sit round the fire and sing. My dad had a wireless which he used to have on for the news and the weather, and when they were finished, it went off. We made our own entertainment, you see.

I remember when I was seven years old; my mum said to me, 'You're a big girl now. You can come and help me upstairs'. I think to myself, I started housework when I was seven. I used to do the errands as well.

We moved into Congerstone and I liked Congerstone because I had a lovely big room as it was a large house. The kitchen was ever so big and at night when Mum used to be dishing up the dinner, Dad would clear the grate and build it up with a nice lump of wood and coal and a bit of slack and that would be getting nice and hot while we had dinner. I didn't seem to be frightened of the dark and anyone who wanted to go to the lavatory, I had to take them up the garden, and it used to be cold, you know, and there was only a candle for light.

We had an aunt and uncle who lived down Barton Lane, at Congerstone, and they had seven children. The eldest girl was twelve when her mum died, too young to look after the family, so the family got split up. Some of the children were adopted and Lottie and Brian came to live with us.

Jim outside his shop - J W Lampard & Son - established 1926

'THESE TWO MEN IN WHITE COATS SAID THEY HAD COME FOR BRIAN AND THEY HAD GOT TO TAKE HIM AWAY'

Well the NSPCC were always calling round, I can see the NSPCC man now a tall thin man he was. He kept coming and saying we were overcrowded and I don't remember how we slept, but Brian slept with the lads, and Lottie slept with me and Madge.

Anyway, we had this Christmas party at school. Santa hadn't been round with the presents and one of the teachers came and said to me that I was wanted at the gate. I went down and there was something like an ambulance and these two men in white coats said they had come for Brian and they had got to take him away. I asked them if my parents knew. They said they didn't know about that but they had got this form. I said, but he hasn't had his Christmas present, and they said they would wait. Well, he got his little present, but he didn't want to go. It was absolutely dreadful! They put him in this van and they took him to an orphanage, at Christmas of all times. I tell you, it put a chip on that lad's shoulder for ever. He has never been the same lad since. He does keep in touch, although he lives in Canada now. He sends me a Christmas card. I am in touch with his sister, Lottie, who lives in Atherstone.

We lived in Bosworth at the corner house, where Softleys is now. We moved there from Congerstone. I remember the day we moved, as it was the garden fête at Congerstone. They had a fancy dress parade and my sister Madge and I were in this fancy dress parade. Madge was a nurse and she won the first prize. My dad told us to catch the bus home. We didn't have watches and we kept asking people the time because we knew we had to catch the bus. There were only about three buses. They used to come up from Ashby and they came round the villages to get into Bosworth. I often wonder now how my mother managed to get all the stuff packed up when she had only had her baby a month. He was born on 22nd June and we came to Bosworth on

22nd July. The next morning we took the kiddies a walk to get out of my mother's way. We went to the mill dam, towards Carlton, and Dinky fell in the dam. Madge got in to fetch him out and then she was sinking so I had to lie flat on the floor with Sonny holding onto my feet and eventually we managed to pull them both out.

'I NEARLY GOT ABDUCTED BY THE WAKE PEOPLE'

We stayed at the house in Bosworth for just over twelve months. Had the door been on the Square, we might have stayed longer, but it was on the side, on Station Road. Jean, my youngest sister, ran straight out of the door into the road and into a car. We had to take her to the Royal because she had damaged her knee and when my dad came home, he said, 'I had an idea that this would happen. We are not stopping here'. We had the chance of a house in Coton next to the Priory.

Mum let Mervine, a nine year old girl, take Madge and I to the Wake. We were walking round looking at the boats and everything so pretty. There was this box with all these lovely balls in it. I remember standing looking at all these balls and, oh, they were such pretty colours. I don't know whether I was picked up or I walked there, or what happened, but the next thing I remember I am sitting in this caravan. I haven't got any shoes and socks on. I don't remember them taking my shoes and socks off. I was sitting there and this woman came towards me. She had this pretty little plate and I could see that there were four new potatoes on it and that they were cold. I knew they were cold and I didn't want cold potatoes but she was trying so hard to push them onto me that I started to cry. I said I wanted to go home. Well, I didn't know where my shoes and socks were and I don't know how long I was in there. Of course I started to scream, and apparently Madge and Mervine had looked for me and couldn't find me and so they went back thinking that I had gone home. My dad had come home from work and she had to tell him that they couldn't find me and apparently he didn't bother going round the fair but went straight to where the caravans were. He could hear me crying and came in and piggybacked me home. I didn't have my shoes and socks. Apparently there was a girl at Norton whose name was Sybil Thorp, and she disappeared when the Wake people were there. She was never found and they say that if they hadn't got any children and saw a kid that looked pretty healthy she just disappeared, and they never did see her again. I nearly got abducted.

David Salmon writes: We lived at Sedgemere which was the site of the old brickyard. Frank Bouskell bought the piece of ground from Squire Scott for £97 for five acres. Originally the house was thatched but it was burnt to the ground in March, 1936. I believe a spark from a passing train had set it on fire. Frank Bouskell couldn't afford the insurance at the time. My father paid for the bungalow to be built by Freemans of Hinckley.

Sedgemere, Station Road

'IF YOU PLANTED CELERY ON TOP OF IT YOU GOT CELERY LIKE OAK TREES!'

Gordon Earp –We bathed in the old zinc bath by the open fire and range. We had a pump in the kitchen to pump the water. My mother had an old mangle and we used to help her do the washing and mangling on washday. It took us all day to do the washing on Mondays, in those days. She did it with a dolly and punched it up and down.

There was no electricity, it was all cooking by the range and the primus stove, and we had candles to go to bed with, which blew out with the draught on the way up the stairs. There were fireplaces upstairs but we didn't have fires in them. We had attics and there were fireplaces in the attics where we had boys living that were working on the farm, in those days. We didn't have electricity until about 1936 or something like that. Dad had to pay for it to come up to the Tollgate but before that we had oil lamps in the house.

For soft water we had a pump behind the door in the back kitchen. The water came from a well that collected all the water off the house. We had to clean the well out every now and again, as it used to whiff a bit. In earlier days we used to dig a trench in the garden and tip the contents of the earth closets in there. If you planted celery on top of it you got celery like oak trees!

Kay Palmer – The small houses had a pump but the large houses, like the Dower House and shops, had piped water. There was a pump at the bottom of Barton Road supplying a lot of the cottages there; it must have been hard work. There was one in Park Street, at the junction with Church Walk, outside the Primary School and there is still one outside Rainbow Cottage, Sutton Lane. There was also one in Shenton Lane, a little further down from the cemetery. There was one halfway down on Station Road, more or less opposite those double gates into the Grammar School, and another one further down, opposite to what was the workhouse.

Osbaston House Farm

PROVISIONS

AT ONE TIME BOSWORTH HAD MANY MORE SHOPS THAN IT HAS TODAY AND SOME OF OUR CONTRIBUTORS OFFER MEMORIES OF THE RETAILERS; HAVING SAID THAT, MARKET BOSWORTH IS FORTUNATE IN THE NUMBER OF SHOPS THAT STILL TRADE IN THE TOWN.

Contributors to this section were Barbara Arm, Brian Oakley, Laura Croman, Blanche Symonds, John Thorp, Robert Jarvis and Olive Hicklin.

Barbara Arm writes: On the corner of Church Street and Main Street was Mr Hardwicke's shop. He sold everything from hairpins to dresses and overalls, boots and shoes, rolls of dress material, in particular calico, and many pretty bows and ribbons. Over the road from him was Mr Long, the butcher. He was noted for his famous, tasty pork pies and sausages, also faggots. A pound of sausages would then cost 9d to 1s.

'HOKEY-POKEY, A PENNY A LUMP, THE MORE YOU EAT THE MORE YOU TRUMP'

Further on was Mr Insley, another butcher. In my grandmother's day this shop belonged to Grandfather Trivett. He had a slaughter house, fasting pens et cetera at the back of the Red Lion, which he also owned. At the Red Lion yard he built a brewery where he brewed beer for various other publicans and also delivered barrels of beer to farmers in the neighbourhood. In the row of cottages, where the town houses now are, lived Mrs Farren. She sold fish and chips from her back kitchen.

At the top of Park Street, opposite St Peter's Hall, was Mrs Cooper's shop. Mr Cooper was the local shoe mender and he plied his trade at one end of the shop and at the other end of the counter was Mrs Cooper with the papers, comics and sweets. I remember some of the names: aniseed balls, one penny lucky bags, liquorice shoe laces, sea side pebbles, humbugs and lots more. Further down Park Street was Mr Armson, he was the local carpenter and coffin

maker. Where the Post Office is now, was Mr Perry's bicycle shop. In the summer Mr Musson would come from Hinckley with his pony and trap and bring ice cream. His cornets were one penny but the wafers were two pennies. He would call out:

Hokey-pokey, a penny a lump,
The more you eat the more you jump.

Another version said by Brian Oakley:

Hokey-pokey, a penny a lump,
The more you eat the more you trump.

'THE CO-OP WAS A SMALL SHOP WITH SAWDUST ON THE FLOOR'

Barbara Arm writes: Mr Musson always stopped outside the bicycle shop which was where the Post Office is now. During the winter months he would bring muffins wrapped in beautiful white cloths.

In Main Street was Mr Fletcher and his bake-house adjacent to a private house where Mr Loseby, the solicitor, lived. At the corner of Rectory Lane and Sutton Lane was another baker, Mr Kendrick, but Mother always used Mr Fletcher's shop. Mr Dolman was the manager at the nearby Co-op store in the 1920s.

Across the road from the Co-op, next to the Dixie Arms, were two houses. In one lived Mrs Pollard who sold hats and further along was Mr Headley, the butcher. The Wheatsheaf Inn came next which closed in the 1920s but later became the Central Café. The Post Office was where Familytique, now Dressini, trades. Mr Percy Wright kept the Post Office and also sold books and toys.

In the town there were three butchers and two bakers. At one time, one of the bakers would take people's Sunday dinner to be cooked. Then after Church they would return for their meat and potatoes, which had been put into big tins and cooked after the bread had been taken from the ovens.

Laura Croman – The Co-op was a small shop with sawdust on the floor and facing the door was a marble counter for the bacon, ham and cheese, which was cut with a wire. On the left was a counter selling groceries. The Co-op had a system where, whatever you spent was noted in a book and you got one ticket and one ticket stopped with them. At the end of the quarter, you got what was called 'divvy' and this was much looked forward to, because really it was the only money the women got which was free for them to use as they wished. So I still remember my mother's number, 2937, and that was 'divvy-day' quarterly.

Central Café, Market Place

'MRS BUCKLE-PICKETT WAS THE POSTMISTRESS'

There was also a grocer's run by Mr Beale, whose nickname was Nippy Beale because he was

supposed to nip a raisin in half to get the exact weight. He sold grocery on one side of the counter and facing the door was the sweet section where they had mouth-watering chocolates. The sugar was weighed out into strong blue bags, it wasn't ready packed.

Blanche Symonds writes: Mr Wothers was the blacksmith whose shop was in Park Street and he could make almost anything from iron. The farmers from around brought their horses to him to be shod. The children would stand and watch him and occasionally he would allow the older boys to help blow the bellows.

Hattons, at the Central Café, sold Wimbush cakes on Fridays and we looked forward to them with much anticipation. After the Post Office in the Square, Tebbutt's had a gift shop where Dressini now stands.

At one time, the Post Office was sited on Station Road, now Moxon Cottage, and Mrs Buckle-Pickett was the postmistress. On the HSBC site was Insley's, then Long's butchers and in the Market Place was Williamson's butchers, Miss Shepherd's Weighbridge Antiques, a tearoom, Flude's Saddlery and a branch of Alliance & Leicester.

Top right: Quincey's delivery cart
Bottom right: The Post Office, Market Place
Bottom left: Long's Butchers, delivery cart

'I REMEMBER WE USED TO GET THESE INDIAN GENTLEMEN COMING
ROUND SELLING TEXTILES WHICH WAS NOT TOO COMMON THEN'

John Thorp – Where Bosworth Gallery is now, was Mrs Turner who sold ice cream and cordials, and a little bit of greengrocery. On the corner of Main Street and Park Street, there was a greengrocer's and Stanton's who sold dairy produce and delivered milk. There were several people who came round with mobile shops. Mr Parkin, from Sutton Cheney, used to sell paraffin and he had an open flat lorry from which he sold all his commodities, it was mainly hardware stuff. We also used to get Statham's who came round with greengrocery and groceries. I remember we used to get these Indian gentlemen coming round selling textiles which was not too common then.

Robert Jarvis – I was born at 14 Market Place next door to which was a saddler's shop, run for a few years by Mr Flude. He passed away but his daughter didn't carry on with the saddler's or leather shop. It was then taken over by Henry Batchelor. There was a weighbridge in the Market Place then; over the years the Market Place has changed quite a lot.

Years passed by and the saddler's shop became a second hand shop, then a little café, followed by Mr Bert Williamson's butcher's shop which operated for ten or fifteen years. After it closed Bosworth Gift shop opened but has now ceased trading. Mr and Mrs Pallett opened their front room as a cake shop which was run by Mees Bakers from Ibstock who sold fresh bread and cakes for a short time. As the years went on a wine bar was opened which, for a start, was not very successful, but created a bit of night life, not always appreciated by the people who lived there, but eventually it became Softley's Restaurant.

Olive Hicklin – My dad would give me the money on a Friday. I used to hate Fridays as I had to cycle from Coton to the Co-op to get them (groceries). Everyone seemed to be in there and I had to stand for ages. I thought if I could save enough money I could get the groceries at dinner time on Fridays. So I had this little tin box and I used to try and put as much in it as I possibly could. It was lovely. There would be nobody in the shop and I could get the groceries and put them on my bike and get down home.

'SIR WOLSTAN DIXIE TOOK OVER THE MARKET'

Robert Jarvis – The Wednesday market was initially very good. It was operated by Spooke Erections who laid on free coaches that went round the villages and picked up people and brought them into the market. Bosworth was then very busy. Things seemed to go down hill when Sir Wolstan Dixie took

over the market as it didn't seem quite as well organised. It ran quite well for a little while and then the coaches were cancelled because people were coming in on the free coaches and weren't using the market, they were using the shops in the village. This was not contributing towards the coaches, and as all the stallholders had to pay towards the coaches they were stopped. We are lucky now to get six stalls in Market Bosworth.

HEALTH AND HYGIENE

PRIOR TO 1948 THERE WAS NO NATIONAL HEALTH SERVICE AS WE KNOW IT TODAY. WOMEN WOULD PAY INTO AN INSURANCE SCHEME KNOWN AS THE NURSING ASSOCIATION SCHEME. THIS WOULD PAY FOR THE SERVICES OF THE DISTRICT NURSE; IN MARKET BOSWORTH NURSE BAMFORD HELD THIS ROLE. IT COVERED THE EXPENSE OF CHILDBIRTH AND A TWO WEEK FOLLOW-UP PERIOD. MEN PAID INTO A DOCTORS' SCHEME THROUGH THEIR PLACE OF EMPLOYMENT AND THIS COVERED THE FAMILY. HERE ARE SOME OF THE MEMORIES AND EXPERIENCES OF LOCAL PEOPLE.

Contributors to this section were Barbara Arm, Olive Hicklin, Peter Loseby and Brenda Bates.

Barbara Arm writes: In the autumn we would go blackberrying and one of the remedies made was blackberry vinegar. It was taken to cure a cough. Every spring we had a spoonful of Brimstone and Treacle, this being a mixture of yellow sulphur powder and treacle. It was supposed to clear the skin after winter.

Olive Hicklin – While we were at Norton there was an epidemic of scarlet fever. I think the ones who caught it were taken to Sunnyside Hospital in Hinckley which was the isolation hospital. Of course the school closed.

I remember when we lived at Bosworth Dad had a large carbuncle on his neck. When he came home Mum would have a big bowl and cotton wool ready to bathe the wound but she couldn't do it. It used to make her feel sick, so I had to do it. I used to have to press away and keep pressing with the hot water and cotton wool. I counted the holes in the carbuncle. There were sixteen holes on this great big thing on the back of my dad's neck. He must have been shattered, swinging a seven pound axe all day and I bet it jarred his neck. As soon as he came in Mum would always have a cup of tea for him and I would have to bathe his neck. You would have had time off work today but he had to go to work and I will never forget that time in our life.

The surgery, Beech House, Church Street

'YOU DIDN'T HAVE TO MAKE AN APPOINTMENT, YOU JUST TURNED UP, WENT IN, AND SAW MY SISTER, BRENDA'

Peter Loseby – The surgery, Beech House in Church Street, was also Dr Kelly's home. There was Dr Kelly and Dr Clarke in my memory. It was the last house up on the left in Church Street, before going through the Hospital gates. The surgery and waiting room were through the front door then along a passage and I remember the décor was blue and the floor was red quarry tiles. The waiting room, and what was then the dispensary, was on the left, and the surgery door was just across the passageway.

You went in and, as I recall it, you didn't have to make an appointment, you just turned up, went in, and saw my sister, Brenda, and said you wanted to see the doctor. There was no questioning about why you wanted to see him or what's wrong with you, as there is today. Brenda would get your medical records out, pile them up and then, every so often, take them through to the doctor in the surgery. You would sit there in a fairly small area, it would take about nine maybe ten seats, with people coughing and spluttering over each other.

Brenda was working behind a curtain screen, making up the prescriptions. When it was your turn to see the doctor, you would go across the passageway, up a step and through a door which had red material on, with copper flat-headed nails securing it.

'DR KELLY WOULD SIT THERE, SHOULDERS HUNCHED'

You knocked on the door, of course, and the doctor would shout, 'Come in', and there was a big handle on the door, halfway up, and as a kid it was above my head and then you stepped up into the surgery.

The surgery I always think of as being a bare, dark room, dominated by a large desk behind which the doctor sat. Dr Kelly, an ex-Army doctor, would sit there, shoulders hunched, bent over whilst looking at you as you came through the door. On the immediate right hand wall there was an examination bed and next to that there was a screen.

Along the passage there was a shelf on the wall, probably six feet high, so that kiddies couldn't get at it. That's where the repeat prescriptions were, so you didn't even go in and ask for it, you just took it. In this day and age you can imagine what a furore there would be if drugs were freely available for collection, with nobody monitoring it.

The prescriptions, always in Latin and a doctor's scrawl, were prepared by my sister Brenda. So you hadn't got a clue what he was giving you. She had got various bottles around the wall, brown, blue and green bottles, and she would just make up something in a little white medicine bottle. This was before penicillin, when the main medication used was M&B tablets. If you had an M&B prescription, the initials represented the manufacturer's name, May and Baker, then you knew that the doctor really did think you were ill. Dr Kelly sometimes used to take some convincing about how bad you really were, you always got the impression that he thought you were malingering, until you proved otherwise.

Above: Dr Kelly
Right: Old medicine bottles from the surgery, Church Street

'DR KELLY DID NOT TAKE KINDLY TO BEING CALLED IN OFF THE STREET'

After surgery in the morning, Brenda used to get on her bike and bike over to Newbold where there was another surgery.
When I was young I had several bouts of pneumonia. I well remember, once, mother having to call Dr Kelly in when he was visiting the next door neighbour. Dr Kelly did not take kindly to being called in off the street to look at somebody. Anyway Mother insisted I had gone blue. Dr Kelly looked at me and decided I had got to have six M&Bs in one dose and Mother pointed out that maybe, that was a bit excessive, to which he agreed and reduced it to four. But because these pills were quite large, they were too big anyway for a little kid to take four. So they were crushed and a drop of water added. It tasted awful and I refused to take anymore. Mother was at her wits end because, presumably, I was poorly so Dr Clarke came and he sat down on the side of the bed and said, 'It's like your mother swilling the yard, the M&Bs are the scrubbing brush and then she has to throw lots of water down to wash the dirt away and that's basically the M&Bs, and that's why you have to drink lots and lots of water'. I can't ever imagine Dr Kelly sitting down and explaining

that to a child. Dr Kelly would have said, you take them, full stop. Dr Clarke emigrated to Australia actually and Mother arranged a collection for him. Dr Kelly did not approve of this when Mother took the money to Dr Clarke, because doctors were not there to get tips, they were there to do a job.

Brenda Bates –The doctors used to bring all the prescriptions back to Bosworth and I used to make them up. Somebody from Barlestone would then come and collect them. She had to come on the bus to pick them up and go back on the bus. I had no formal training for this job but I could read the prescriptions in Latin, as I learned Latin at the Grammar School.

Dr Kelly used to come in and make sure I had made up the right prescription. He had his desk across the back wall and he had a set of cupboards at the side, inside which he kept all the lint dressings and cotton wool balls in an enclave. I used to fill it up and take it to the hospital to be sterilized. Sometimes the doctor used to take me to Newbold and sometimes I biked, because he had a surgery there as well.

Background: Prescription shelf

EDUCATION

THERE WAS A TIME WHEN EVERY VILLAGE HAD ITS OWN LITTLE SCHOOL AND THE CHILDREN FELT PART OF ONE BIG FAMILY. SADLY, OVER TIME MANY VILLAGES HAVE COMPLETELY LOST THIS FACILITY AND WAY OF LIFE, BUT NOT BOSWORTH. AS THE BOSWORTH POPULATION HAS GROWN THERE HAVE BEEN MANY CHANGES TO THE EDUCATION SYSTEM AND THE MEMORIES BELOW ILLUSTRATE HOW THIS HAS EVOLVED.

Contributors to this section were Harry Frost, Alwyn Whitney, Ingrid Davison, Mary Vernon, Jill Earp, Barbara Arm, Laura Croman, Olive Hicklin, Joy Crane, Angela Hutton and Alan Eames.

Harry Frost (in an earlier interview) – The Market Bosworth school was founded in 1320. In 1592 'the ould scholehouse' stood north of the schoolmaster's house in what is now the walk up to the church from

Park Street. By the 1590s it had been relocated to the site of the present premises off the Market Place and was refounded by the Dixie family in 1601, later to become known as the Dixie Grammar School. Amongst its noteworthy pupils were William Bradshaw, Thomas Hooker and Samuel Johnson (teacher). Since 1987 the school has been an Independent Grammar School.

St Peter's Primary School, in Park Street, opened in 1848 and moved to the Station Road premises in 1974. The Secondary Modern School opened in Station Road in 1927, was extended in 1934,

and later became the Bosworth High School. The Arms of the Dixie family depict a golden lion on a blue shield and over the shield, the personal crest depicted by the snow leopard, and only later was the 'Bloody Hand of Ulster' added. This crest appears on the gates into St Peter's Primary School in Station Road in a plaque taken from the old Primary School in Park Street.

Top: St Peter's Primary School, Park Street
Right: New Primary School, Station Road

'WE RAISED FUNDS TO GET ST ANNE'S LODGE BUILT THROUGH PLAYS AND CHURCH ASSISTANCE'

Dixie Grammar School from painting by Margaret Atkinson

There were four classes of roughly thirty seven pupils in each class in those days, taught by four teachers, Mrs G C Clarke, myself, Mrs C Hughes and Miss Belcher who had the infants' class. Mrs Clarke had the top-class children down at the Secondary Modern School in Station Road. My aim, throughout 1948, was to get all the children of St Peter's School under one roof. We raised funds to get St Anne's Lodge built through plays and Church assistance and eventually we managed that.

'ONE OF THE OTHER THINGS I FOUGHT FOR AT THAT TIME WAS THE ONE-WAY SYSTEM UP PARK STREET'

Of course, in those days, when walking down through the village to the Modern School no one was allowed to talk. As a Church school, one of the things we had to learn was the Catechism, and a number of children have told me, since they have grown up, how much they enjoyed the repeating of the Catechism. Eventually, I managed to get St Peter's Hall to be used as an extra classroom so that we could have five classes but the trouble was that all school furniture had to be removed at 4 PM, put back in the school, and replaced in the morning.

One of the other things I fought for, at that time, was the one-way system up Park Street, because the playground entrance led straight onto the road. I had that changed so that the children came out into Church Walk rather than onto the main road. Eventually, after 1948 when St Anne's Lodge was built, we had yet another classroom, so we were growing greatly in numbers, particularly after the other village schools closed.

Alwyn Whitney – During the years when Mr Harry Frost was the head teacher at the Primary School, the classes met in three different areas; this was before the building of the Station Road Primary School. St Anne's Lodge on Church Walk was used for the reception class, the Parish Room adjoining the Old Rectory was occupied by the other infant classes and the Park Street School was for the junior children. The three sections of the school only came together at lunch time when they ate in St Peter's Hall, after which, if the weather was good, they would be taken to the Parish Field to play. Another time when the

whole school met was for the weekly Wednesday morning service in the church. In 1968 the four junior school classes moved into the new building on Station Road and the three infant classes came together in the old Park Street School. St Anne's Lodge was no longer needed. St Anne's Lodge was a tunnel-shaped Nissen hut with a corrugated roof which was very noisy when it rained. There was one heater in the room and one washbasin and toilet for about thirty six children. Outside there was a garden and an apple tree which the children used to like to try and climb, when they were allowed to. By this time the schools at Sutton Cheney, Carlton and Shenton had been closed and children were bussed to school in Bosworth.

Top left: St Anne's Lodge
Right: Mrs Sabine, Harry Frost and Canon Pilling

'ONE LITTLE GIRL IN THE CLASS WHO CAME FROM SHENTON WAS FASCINATED BY THE WATER FROM THE TAPS AND SPENT AGES WASHING HER HANDS'

One little girl in the class who came from Shenton was fascinated by the water from the taps and spent ages washing her hands. They didn't have running water in their house. Another incident that stands out was at the time of the heavy snow during the winter of 1967 when we let the children go home early at 2 PM. The buses came to collect them and as people weren't on the phone we couldn't let the families know. Some children got home and stood outside. A local resident thought it was bad that they were sent home but what could be done? It was better for them to be home than stranded in Market Bosworth.

Angela Hutton – I remember most of my teachers at the Secondary Modern School. Mr Long taught science, he was very strict; Mrs Long, I believe, taught history; Mr and Mrs Wallace, geography and scripture. Mr Curzon taught mathematics, he had a temper and would throw the board rubber across the room at pupils if they didn't behave and send them out of the class room. One particular student seemed to aggravate him because he talked a lot in class. Mrs Hardy taught domestic science and I remember winning a competition for the best Christmas cake that I had made in class. We also had dancing lessons and we learned the waltz, quickstep and rock and roll. The tune I remember dancing to, for rock and roll, was 'Peggy Sue' by Buddy Holly. Mr Jenkins was the Headmaster for the latter part of my time at this school. The name of the school was changed from the Secondary Modern to the High School. Pupils were segregated into classes by ability – A, B, C and, I believe, R for the slower learners. Each class had a form teacher and there were form position ratings for pupils, either each term or academic year. Pupils' names would be displayed on a list on the classroom wall as to how they had performed over the range of subjects. I remember feeling very proud as I was always in the top three, sometimes coming first!

'AT BREAK TIMES WHEN CHILDREN HAD THEIR MILK MR FROST OPERATED A TUCK SHOP'

Alwyn Whitney – In 1974 the whole school finally came together on the Station Road site. Mr Harry Frost only had the school under one roof for the last five years of his headship. He had been at the school since 1949 and retired in 1979. By the time he retired there were ten classes at the school, two of which were in temporary classrooms. Mr Frost produced plays every year. He wrote the plays and Mrs Vernon provided the music. Year 5 children would be involved in the music and Year 6 were the actors in the plays. On Tuesday and Thursday afternoons Mr Frost would take the older children to St Peter's Hall for drama lessons. After his retirement drama continued under the leadership of other members of the staff and in 1980 the school took part in A Leicestershire Tapestry, performed by many county schools

at the Haymarket Theatre. St Peter's acted and danced the story of the Battle of Bosworth.

At break times when children had their milk Mr Frost operated a tuck shop and he actually sold the biscuits et cetera to the children himself. This way he got to know them, as he did at lunch times, when he would eat alongside the children.

Changes took place in secondary education in 1969 when the Secondary Modern School became the High School and the Dixie Grammar School moved to Desford and became Bosworth College. There was no longer an 11+ examination as all children went to new comprehensive schools.

The cast of the school play - Hansel and Gretel 1951

'THE BOYS WOULD SNEAK OUT AND OPEN THE GATE TO THE VERY INFREQUENT MOTOR VEHICLES, UNTIL ONE GOT KILLED AND THEN A STOP WAS PUT TO THAT'

Laura Croman – My school was up Park Street, St Peter's School, and it was the only one until the year I started (1926). Part of the central school was being built down Station Road. My teacher was Miss Tapp, a lovely woman. The room was heated by a coke burning stove with a large guard round it so the children who had to walk from Coton and Osbaston, and got wet clothes in the process, could put their clothes round there to dry during school time. The playground was very small but we could go out onto the road that led up to the church. In the middle of the road, Church Walk, was a pump and because the children played with it Mrs Graver, who was the widow of the previous headmaster, had it chained up. Just higher up from the school was a gate across the road, which kept the deer on the Park; the boys would sneak out and open the gate to the very infrequent motor vehicles, until one got killed and then a stop was put to that.

When I moved up from Miss Tapp's class to Miss Sutton's which was the only other class in the school, at that time, I earned tuppence a week for using a button hook to button up her, what was called in those days, Russian boots, boots that came up to the knee, leather boots. I used to button them up before she went home every night and unbutton them in the morning when she came in.

Ingrid Davison – I can remember being at school in St Anne's Lodge which was where the Rectory is now. It was a Nissen hut and I can remember the alphabet on the wall and the little chairs. I know my memory hasn't failed me because the lamp-post is still there in the corner and I used to run round and round it.

My favourite class was Mr Heathcote's, when I must have been ten or eleven. He used to tell us fantastic history stories and I was gripped, and ever since then I have loved history. I studied it through school and when I went to teacher training college it was my subsidiary subject. I still love it now, because of Mr Heathcote.

Church Walk with Jane Vernon

'LARGE AND FEROCIOUS YOUNGSTERS CALLED US THE NIPPERS'

Mary Vernon writes: She was in charge of the school music and Mr Frost was in charge of plays. Music was mostly singing and the school had a small orchestra. Mrs Vernon taught the children to play the recorder in the dinner hours, which they loved, and they had flutes, clarinets and triangles. The school only had three flutes so the parents bought the others. Fortunately Mrs Vernon's husband was a great flautist so he looked after all the instruments. The orchestra played at school concerts and plays. St Peter's Church was absolutely packed with parents and friends when they had Christmas carol

services in the church. They would have just a small choir and some instruments.

Mr Frost used to write a new play every year with singing and dancing organized by Mrs Vernon. Performances were at Christmas or during the spring term and were always very good.

Alan Eames writes: Those who can remember the Infant Nursery School, in Park Street, in the early fifties, will recall that it was nothing more than a single roomed Nissen hut about halfway along the pathway from the street to St Peter's Church. It was on the left of this path and faced a wall and, to us, mysterious door leading to Mr Beck's new bungalow. This asphalt road was our playground, though we were very limited to the distance that we could stray downhill towards the big school. Down there were large and ferocious youngsters who called us 'the nippers' and chased us when they could. Mr Frost, the Headmaster, banned this derogatory term officially, which, of course, only encouraged it the more!

There was a wall and another gate towards the church. We peeped in there and saw the spire of St Peter's a great distance away. The doorway was dark and fearsome. In the corner of the gate and walls was an iron lamp-post around which you could hook your arm and run in circles until you were very dizzy and often sick.

Mrs Sabine was a slim lady with very dark and very straight hair, an exception in the age of the perm. We were all very respectful of her and thought her formidable. We were also very fond of her and generally thought her a kind person. Sometimes we would bring her wild flowers, which we knew she liked, or snowdrops in a bowl in the winter.

Above: Mrs Vernon, centre front, with some of the staff from St Peter's Primary School
Right: The entrance to the churchyard, Church Walk

'FOR WRITING, SLATES WERE USED, ENCASED IN A LITTLE WOODEN FRAME'

After prayers we embarked on a daily ritual. A, we said, says a, B says b, and C says c. This continued, as one would expect, until Z said zzz. We were very soon quite sure what they all said and armed with this useful information began to read Beacon Book 1, progressing to 2, et cetera, until 7 or 8. To help us in this quest for knowledge, a student teacher painted a fruit or article against each letter of the alphabet on the wall. She was a good artist and the paintings were very realistic. The letters were perfectly formed and the black paint shone and glistened as she worked. We were fascinated. Around the clock at the end of the hut she inscribed the words Tempus Fugit (*time flies*). What this meant we did not then know, but we know now and we know that it was true.

For writing, slates were used, a thick cold and smooth slate that was encased in a little wooden frame. This was near the end of the days of slates and many were old and broken even then. A square slate pencil was used like a crayon and white marks were made; these could easily be wiped off with a damp cloth and the clean slate was ready again. Sadly, life isn't that simple and the slates are gone.

There was sand, plasticine and clay. The sand was in trays and got on the floor, the clay also, this was a very clinging and sticky substance, extremely messy. Plasticine was better and came in bright colours but after a week or two all became combined into murky balls with the occasional rainbow streak left. We made long rolls and twisted them into many shapes. It had a peculiar smell and got under your fingernails.

Most days somebody was sick or wet their pants. Teachers were used to this and had a defence of mop and bucket or a box of sawdust which was tipped over the sick and stayed there, a fearful splodge which we avoided carefully. The offending sick-producer or pant-wetter was mollified and sat away from us in smelly discomfort until mothers appeared at midday.

'TEMPUS FUGIT - WHAT THIS MEANT WE DID NOT THEN KNOW'

The Infants' was a happy place. We painted our pictures and sang our songs and seemed to spend at least one lifetime there but in fact it was less than a year and soon time to go on to the big school along the path, where the huge coke heap was and the noisy children; another world to be faced and conquered.

Mrs Fisher was the teacher in charge of Class 3, which was located in the crosswise room at the east end of the junior school building. One door led to the boys' playground at the back, another to the small girls' playground at the front. We sat in twos at wooden desks with lids and pot inkwells, though I don't think that ink was allowed until Class 2. More Beacon Books appeared and we learnt simple letter formation and sums of a basic standard.

Mrs Fisher had straight white hair and seemed much older than Mrs Sabine; she came from Newbold Verdon. At the end of each day she would produce a very large thick volume called 'The Omnibus' and read us a story.

'WE WOULD GET ON, CLUTCHING OUR LEATHER SATCHELS'

While winter had seemed to reign supreme during my stay at the Infants', summer was in charge at Class 3. I can't think that this was really so; maybe the fact that the Junior School had central heating was significant. Lucky were the people who sat by a radiator or a pipe; as well as being warm, these could be tapped or parts unscrewed.

Footwear for boys remained boots, with hobnails just like the Bisto Kid. Socks were woolly and fell down to the ankles unless supported by elastic garters; too tight and they were painful and left red rings below the knee, too loose and down came the socks. The hobnails meant that you could slide on the asphalt; squat down on the haunches and hold up two hands and two other boys would pull you along at speed. When the nails wore out, Father would upend the boots on a cobbler's iron-last and hammer in some more.

When playtime was over, Mr Heathcote would blow a whistle and we would quickly form lines to go into class. Kicking the coke heap was frowned on and would result in punishments. We were aware of the cane by now and there were legends of its use. I don't recall it ever actually being used in the five years that I was at St Peter's, but the thought of it was enough to bring us into line.

We were now travelling to school by bus from Osbaston and Cadeby. The bus company was Clarence Coaches from Barton in the Beans. The driver was either Cyril, who was short, plump and jolly, or Walter who was thin and gloomy. Sometimes there was a third

mysterious driver who we thought was called Clarence. The bus of this time was a remarkable vehicle. It produced a great squealing whine; a most distressing sound which redoubled at the slightest incline. It was blue and the radiator and headlamps gave it a sad, shocked expression. It would appear at the bottom road into Osbaston on the A447, as my cousin Jane Vernon and I waited at the top lane and watched it grind its way very slowly towards us. We would get on, clutching leather satchels and the bus then carried on to Cadeby to pick up the Prices, Michael Baker and Edward Deacon. It already contained the Jinks from Osbaston Tollgate.

School dinners were provided at a cost of 3s 9d per week (18p), though they had been 2s 6d. We were formed into long crocodiles and led, hand in hand, to the Secondary Modern School; down Park Street and through a narrow way. Folding tables and benches were set out and dollops of boiled cabbage or carrots, stew (thick or thin) and mashed potato. The dinners had a remarkable odour which I have never smelled since, except once in a canteen, such is the evocativeness of the sense of smell that all the memories of the thick, white plates and aluminium tureens came flooding back. The custard came in tall, white jugs and was extremely foamy and rather thin. I suppose it was made from powder, like the potatoes. Class 3 ended in 1952 and the next class was Class 2 with Mr Heathcote.

Most of us were somewhat in awe of the teacher in Class 2, Mr Heathcote. For some reason, I've never known why, we called him Spud.

Background: A Clarence coach

'THE DEAR OLD GENTLEMAN WOULD GIVE HIM SIXPENCE'

It was Mr Heathcote who blew the whistle in the school playground and made us form neat lines, on the double. Mr Heathcote would shout at us if we made him cross and on the, fortunately, rare occasions when fighting broke out it was he who dragged the opponents apart. But fights did happen. A cry of, 'Fight! Fight!' would go up and in a few seconds, a thick circle of onlookers would crowd around the action. Boys formed gangs and had strong territorial ambitions. I was in Peter Paget's gang which was not a very successful organisation.

Mr Heathcote was very keen on Old Norse legends. At the end of the school day tales were told of Loki, the god of fire and, particularly, Thor whose drinking capacity was so great that his thirst wasn't quenched until the drinking horn was connected to the ocean and the sea level fell, exposing the land. These pagan gods took our fancy and were in strong competition with the Christian education that we received.

On Tuesday mornings we were led to St Peter's Church to sing hymns, pray and listen to a short address by the then incumbent, Canon Payne. The Canon had a very low and weak, droning voice and appeared to us to be extremely old. His hair was white and as he stood by the pulpit we found it quite impossible to hear what he said. After a period of what seemed several hours, he would suddenly point at a boy and ask him to come up, when the lad arrived the dear old gentleman would give him sixpence.

By now St Peter's Hall was constructed and our school dinners were provided in there. The disapproval of salt continued, as did our desire for custard. Chips did not exist, only mashed potato, carrots and cabbage with meat pie or pudding or corned beef. Eggs were rare and expensive and would appear, perhaps, twice a year in a salad. Jelly was common, as was rice pudding, tapioca and sago. The post-war government, mindful of vitamin deficiencies did provide rose-hip syrup which we rapidly stirred into the sago to make a nasty pink mush. I still do this if I get the chance, though my wife says it is disgusting.

'WE NOW HAD PENS, INITIALLY

WOODEN ONES, DIPPED INTO

THE INKWELLS'

We now had pens, initially wooden ones, dipped into the inkwells. Ink monitors with metal jugs on long handles filled the wells daily. This was all extremely messy. With great care we formed upper and lower case letters and copied from the blackboard. Fountain pens were in use but not biros and felt tips had not been invented. One could get a severe shock from sucking the end of ones Platignum pen for some time to discover ones mouth, lips, and end of nose were indelibly black or blue for several days.

The pant-wetters had now almost ceased, though the sick-producers continued for some time. Sweets were eaten as much as possible; rarely crisps. Crisps were much thicker and chewier then and of course, always had the little blue bag. Aniseed balls, liquorice, sherbet fountains and various boiled sweets were the usual fare though chews, in a variety of lurid and probably carcinogenic colours, were now appearing in the shops.

'WE HAD TO FIGHT OUR WAY UP OSBASTON LANE BETWEEN HIGH DRIFTS'

I remember Class 2 as a winter class. There was plenty of snow and we had to fight our way up the narrow Osbaston lane between high drifts. After a few days the snow in the playground became hammered down by the children's feet and it was possible to make slides. Teachers today would probably become hysterical if slides appeared. Steady sliding over a patch of snow, over two or three days, would produce a long ribbon of totally slippery, glassy ice. We would run as fast as we could and launch ourselves onto one end of

the blackboard. In one corner he drew a line; so did we. He then drew another line; we did too. We then did exactly the same in all the other squares. This was continued until a chequerboard pattern appeared. We admired this greatly as it looked just like the wallpaper in the sitting room at home.

Mr Frost fished some of us out of Class 2 and taught us two mornings a week in St Peter's Hall. We vacated the Hall at midday for the dinner tables to be set up and waited for the

'MR FROST WOULD COME OUT AND SPRINKLE SALT OVER THE CHERISHED SLIDE, TO OUR DISMAY AND DISGUST'

the slide then travel at speed to the other end and hopefully, keep on our feet. At last, it would become so dangerous that Mr Frost would come out and sprinkle salt over the cherished slide, to our dismay and disgust.

Where our teachers came from or where they went to after school we did not know. In the early days we believed that they were there all the time. But we did know that Mr Heathcote lived away because he had a most remarkable bicycle with an engine around the middle of the back wheel.

We painted using poster paints. Free expression was hardly heard of in those days and we did not produce weird abstract splodges of colour to take home to mother. No, we were given a sheet of grey paper, which we carefully divided up into squares. Mr Heathcote produced the same squares on

delivery of the dinner in the big aluminium pots. The dinner ladies, Mrs Granger and Mrs Gamble, would open the pots to ladle out the material inside.

The year passed. We learnt more copywriting, some geography and history and studied Bible stories. Like most children we had by now developed collecting crazes for stamps, lapel badges, trains et cetera. My friend, John Lancaster, had a wonderful train set of which I was very jealous, as I had an inferior one that could hardly struggle around the track. John's father was signalman down at Bosworth Station but the family lived in the Timber Fireproof bungalows near Churchill's factory. I would visit John to play and usually we would get to sit in the box, amid all the wonderful levers and bells and watch the coal trains steaming south from the North West Leicester coalfield.

'WE COULD QUITE FREELY GO DOWN TO THE SHOPS'

We were now aged eight or nine and it was time to go to Class 1, the other side of the big glass screen where the piano was and the radio. Mrs Clarke was, or seemed to be, an elderly lady with grey hair in two 'bangs' on either side, the 'wireless', as my mother called it. She was our teacher. Craven A was the cigarette that Mrs Clarke smoked during the day; nobody seemed at all concerned about this.

Class 1 was the room where morning assembly and prayers took place. The glass screen was rolled back by two youngsters and Mr Frost would read from the book, 'Prayers and Hymns for Junior Schools'. On our birthdays we could choose a hymn and the boys would generally opt for, 'When a knight won his spurs in the stories of old'.

We were allowed remarkable freedom in Class 1. We could quite freely go down to the shops, as long as Mr Frost knew. We would walk down Park Street past Thorp's rather forbidding house, past Clem Phillips' blacksmith's shop, with the bright forge glowing inside and old Clem hammering away, and sometimes Mrs Phillips would be on the step and glare at us; across Barton Lane and by the old Post Office, kept by Mr Jackson, to Tebbutt's sweet shop where the gob-stoppers were. There was little traffic, an occasional Gibson's bus or black car or sometimes the extraordinary electric tram used by Sir Thomas Cope of Osbaston Hall. Sir Thomas would sit crouched over the wheel with deerstalker and military white moustache, gazing fixedly ahead and the tram would whine its way up the hill; he had been to the bank and to collect groceries and other vital necessities for life in the gloomy, decaying mansion.

On a sunny day in May, in the afternoon, Mr Frost would decide that we should not be indoors. We would ask if we could go for a walk and he would say, 'Yes of course but don't be away too long'. The responsible children were then allowed to walk down Barton Lane to Stoney Brook and back. It was perfectly safe then.

'MRS PHILLIPS WOULD BE ON THE STEP AND GLARE AT US'

The copywriting was nearly over now. We had mastered long division and multiplication, stones, pounds and ounces, yards, feet and inches, pounds, shillings and pence. All the tables could be recited (very useful for quick mental calculations) by heart, as could the litany of twelve pence one shilling, eighteen pence one and sixpence et cetera, up to 120 pence - ten shillings. We commenced upon fractions; lowest common denominators, highest common multiples. We could multiply and add them and attack problems of the classic type, that is, if ten men mow a field in two hours, how long would it take twelve men?! We were now ready for the 11+, that sadly divisive exam that sundered friend from friend and dictated your future life for the sake of the assessment of a child at eleven years old. But we were fortunate at St Peter's; fully half of the class would pass and go to the Dixie Grammar.

'IT WAS AS HAPPY A SCHOOL AS ANY ONE COULD WISH FOR'

Mr Frost was keen on plays for children. He was a legend in the district. Each year he would write a new one, to be performed in St Peter's Hall, the proceeds to pay for the school trip to Dudley Zoo and for a Christmas party with a genuinely good present for each child. Santa would hand out the coveted parcels and a high tea of salmon paste sandwiches, cakes and, of course, jelly would appear. Crêpe paper decorations and twisted streamers would be put up in each classroom.

gate. It was on to the secondary schools, in particular, for me, to the Dixie Grammar where a quite different regime from that at St Peter's was practiced.

St Peter's was as happy a school as any one could wish for, full of consideration and love. Whether it was before its time I don't know; I don't think it useful to consider it in these terms, goodness and kindness are timeless after all.

'SHE WAS QUITE HANDY WITH A STICK WITH US VILLAGE CHILDREN. I HAD IT A

TIME OR TWO AS YOUNG AS I WAS'

In class, furtive notes declaring undying love would be passed along the rows of desks. They would be folded many times or screwed into balls; sometimes little packets containing sticky chews would accompany them. Certain Cromans, Coolings and Stantons, but, unfortunately not Veros, were responsible for this. Others names now also come to mind; the Boughtons and Melias, Stephen Kelly, Peter Ebsworth, Sandra Ethel May Head; where did they all go? By mid-July the end of Primary School had arrived. No more sitting behind the railings of the front playground waiting for the bus; no more chatting to the two old gentlemen from the old people's home (we called them tramps!); the thin one with no teeth and the fat one called Percy. No more cricket in the field by the Remembrance Garden against Clem Phillips' wrought iron

Olive Hicklin – I remember the school teacher at Norton juxta Twycross, Mrs Nesbitt. She was tall, thin, with dark hair and quite strict. I think all the children were in the one room. She had a coke stove which she had to look after herself, and a chair at the side of it. She was quite handy with a stick with us village children. I had it a time or two as young as I was. She and her own three children lived in the School House which had a porch and was on the edge of the playground. If they were naughty, the belt which used to hang in the porch was fetched and she used to belt her own three. First time I ever saw navy blue knickers. But she was really a lovely, lovely woman. I think if I had been with her until I was eleven, I would have been better educated because she made you listen; she made you take notice.

'TO CATCH THE BUS WE HAD TO WALK THROUGH FOUR FIELDS IN WELLINGTONS AND THEN CHANGE SHOES AT A HOUSE IN BARLESTONE'

Jill Earp — I started Thurlaston School at five but my brother didn't start until he was seven. This was because living down the fields, we had to go over a brook to school or go all the way round to the bridge. We went with some other children from the next farm. I went with him every day and we used to take our sandwiches in a tin box which we ate, in what we called the bogey hole. It was just a room with very high windows, you couldn't see out, just a darkish room with a stove in the middle of the floor. In the winter we were allowed to take a potato to put in the stove so we could have a hot jacket potato for lunch.

We had a very strict headmistress. We were all terrified of her as she used to shout and yell at everybody but when you look back she was very good.

Barbara Arm writes: Up to the age of eleven I was at the Market Bosworth Infant School in Park Street. To get to the school from Osbaston we were taken in a governess cart, we called it the 'tub'. We were taken up for 9 o'clock in the morning. The small children from the age of five from the village, walked to school, either to Bosworth or Cadeby, but mostly to Bosworth. They usually carried a small cotton bag made by their mothers, in which they carried their lunch. They walked in all weathers and sometimes, if it was raining, Mother would tell us to make room for them to ride in our 'tub'.

When I was eleven years old I went to Leicester Convent on a bus from Barlestone at 8 o'clock. To catch the bus we had to walk through four fields in wellingtons and then change shoes at a house in Barlestone. We had a lantern to carry at night to see our way through the fields. The older girls were sent to Ashby Girls' Grammar School. To get to Ashby they left home on cycles and caught the milk train from Bosworth which took them to Ashby.

Joy Crane — At the Grammar School in Bosworth, we were doing a maths lesson one day and I had been notoriously bottom of maths all the time. Mr Webb used to sympathise with me, he was the maths teacher, and one day one of the boys sniggered at me because I couldn't answer a simple question. Mr Webb just turned to him and said, 'Harvey can you milk a cow?' and he said, 'No.' Mr Webb said, 'Well don't snigger at somebody who can.' And later on he told me that the only hope for me was to find a fella who could do maths, and there is one in lower five, or whatever class it was he was in, you ought to get together with him. Well two or three years later I did!

Governess cart

RELIGION

THERE HAS BEEN A CHRISTIAN PRESENCE IN THE TOWN, CERTAINLY SINCE SAXON TIMES, WHEN A SAXON CHURCH OCCUPIED THE PRESENT SITE OF ST PETER'S CHURCH. THE PRESENT BUILDING DATES FROM THE 14TH AND 15TH CENTURIES, THE TOWER BEING THE OLDEST PART OF THE CHURCH.

Contributors to this section were Maurice Harris, Robert Leake, Cyril Smith, Harry Frost, John Ensor, Pat and George Cooling, and Diana Morgan.

Maurice Harris – The original Independent Chapel was in Park Street opposite the Forge. The Baptist Church at that time was in Station Road to the rear of Nos 9 and 11 and now forms the out-houses for these properties. It moved to Barton Road in 1848 and was later to become the Free Church. This was built on the Dixie Estate, on the site of a carpenter's cottage, which is now known as the Chapel House Meeting Rooms. Interestingly, Sir Willoughby Dixie the 8th Baronet, a Catholic, refused to give them any ground. They pestered and pestered him until he agreed to allow them the use of the empty carpenter's cottage. Dixie told them to go and mark out a piece of ground and providing that access was available to the carpenter's cottage and sheds to the left of the property, the church could be built there. When they built it, in order to allow as large a church as possible, the south wall was one yard longer than the north wall!

In 1931 the Estate went into liquidation. In the Sale Catalogue the church in Barton Road was included in the sale as no deeds had been exchanged. So the Barton Group of churches then had to buy the land for something like £350 and for some reason, they decided to recoup that money but as Bosworth could not raise the money, the church was closed. One of the reasons that they had decided to close the church was that in the roof was a 5ft 6ins roundel with a gas mantle, a very ornate plasterwork, which appeared to be falling away from the ceiling. The Barton Group deemed that it wasn't safe for the Bosworth people to sit under because it might fall. I have seen Minutes that say that the people of Bosworth must pray before services that it wouldn't fall down on them before the service was finished! The church was closed until 1949. During the war, the Air Raid Precaution (ARP) Wardens had it as a reporting centre and the local authority used it to store dustbins and materials that the council had removed from their buildings in Station Road which had been taken over by Churchill Components. They were a bombed out Coventry firm who made aeroplane parts and had been brought to Bosworth because it was a safer environment.

'WHEN EVENTUALLY THE CHAPEL WAS TAKEN OVER, IT WAS COMPLETELY DERELICT'

In 1947 a group of people got together to form a Non-Conformist Church, deciding to form a united church for Baptists, Methodists and Congregationalists, as together they could form a Free Church. For the first two years they met at the rear of the Central Café, in the Wheatsheaf Courtyard, in an upper room above the old stables, now the coffee house. Then in 1949 the Church persuaded the Barton Group to sell the church building. They refused, but said that we could have it on a peppercorn rent which was done for a number of years. Two men had spent a week trying to get the roundel down. The roof had not been maintained since 1931 and the windows had all blown in so when, eventually, the chapel was taken over it was completely derelict.

Pat Cooling – On one occasion when going to Evensong with my grandma, who was very, very Victorian, there was a parade of the Home Guard up to the church. They had a special Evensong every so often and I happened to go with my grandma on such an evening and I daren't move! I was probably about four to five years old at the time, just having started Sunday School. I normally went with my sister and I didn't know the whys and wherefores of Sunday School. Once I was talking, which I thought you could, and Canon Payne came down and said to Rosemary, my sister, 'If you can't keep Patricia quiet you will have to take her home'.

That was my first memory of Sunday School! We didn't have prizes at Sunday School, all we had were birthday stamps and stamp albums. Every week you got a stamp for your album and for a birthday you got a birthday stamp. That was it. I enjoyed the singing. I was always interested and eventually joined the choir and have been a member for sixty odd years. The choir was all male at one time, but when Mrs Stenton came and the men had gone to the war, I think that's when the ladies were allowed into the choir.

Top: Drawing of Free Church, Barton Road
Above right: Canon Payne with Church Choir, early 1950s.

'I WILL CALL YOU A LIAR'

In 1954 Canon Pilling arrived. He was like a breath of fresh air after Canon Payne, being different altogether. He got a lot of youngsters into Church at the time so he really changed things around a bit. Canon Pilling was very funny and very emotional. He could be crying one minute and making you laugh the next, but there again you had to sit still. He wouldn't have any hanky-panky, you had to sit and listen to his sermons!

The sermon that Canon Pilling would give at weddings always seemed to contain a particular sentence: 'and if I see you in the street in three months time and you say you haven't had an argument, **I will call you a liar**', and it rang round the church.

George Cooling — We had May parades and garden fêtes when the May Queen travelled on the back of Mr Beck's lorry which would go round Bosworth. At the summer Church Garden Fête they always used to have the Barlestone Brass Band playing.

Robert Leake writes: In St Peter's Church tower there are eight bells, two dated 1624 and 1630 although two others could be earlier! Bells were rung to announce the times of prayers to the people. One from 1660 was given by the Dixie family, 'for the most happy return of King Charles II' after the Cromwell Commonwealth interlude. The three treble bells, added in 1950, are mentioned on the World War II Memorial Plaque to the left of the doors to the choir vestry in the church.

John Ensor writes: In 1950 three new bells were added to the five existing ones at St Peter's Church which had been taken down for restoration and then re-hung as part of a World War II memorial to local people who had lost their lives.

An Appeal for a Peal

Dear Friends,

This year on Easter Sunday, when all Churches in the land ring out their joyful message that "Christ is Risen," your bells—the bells of St. Peters, Market Bosworth—will be silent.

Experts have examined the present bells and have advised that if ringing is continued a collapse might occur at any time.

Your Church Council have carefully considered the problem and have resolved to go forward with the Restoration of Five bells at an estimated cost of £954, adding two smaller bells and executing repairs to the tower if the funds permit.

A provisional order has been placed with the bell founders and this is dependent on at least £500 being raised before December this year.

It is hoped that you will be able to help us and will if you can, so please send your portion (however small) to either Mr. John Rolleston, Midland Bank, or to the Rector. All gifts will be gratefully acknowledged.

If the "Appeal for a Peal" goes well, the new Peal on Easter Sunday, 1950, will have a very special message "THANK YOU."

Yours very sincerely,

The Rector and Members of the Church Council.

Easter, 1949.

Church Garden Fête, early 1950s

'THE DOCTOR STORMED OUT OF HIS SURGERY AND STRODE UP THE PATH TO THE CHURCH'

I remember my father was in charge of the removal of the bells from the bell tower to be taken to Taylor's Bell Foundry in Loughborough. They were to have new bearings in the hanging and ringing mechanisms, as I understood it as an eleven year old boy. My father and fellow workers from H Beck & Sons removed the louvered windows on the north side of the tower and then rigged up a winch from ground level to high up in the bell tower. The winch was hand wound and my father stood eighty feet up in the opening directing operations, with absolutely no health and safety regulations involved! I understood that three new bells were added.

Robert Leake writes: For many years Beech House in Church Street was the local doctor's surgery. Dr Gordon Kelly lived there until about 1970 and he used to get very annoyed when the church bells woke him up on a Sunday morning, especially if he had been out all night on an emergency or a baby delivery. His surgery was in the room just beyond the side door porch and patients just queued in the waiting room to be seen in turn. There was no appointment system in those days. He was aware also that the bells could be disturbing to some of the patients at the nearby Bosworth Park Infirmary, now the Bosworth Hall Hotel.

There is a tale that one evening, while a bell practice was going on, the doctor stormed out of his surgery and strode up the path to the church, switched off the tower lights, tugged at the bell ringers' signal rope, went home and wrote a strong letter of complaint to the Rector. Well this is a true story, because a copy of the reply sent to Dr Kelly by the Rector on December 1st 1953 has been found. In it the Rector, Canon Francis R C Payne, explained that he called a full meeting of the bell ringers together with the Church Wardens and Mr John Rolleston, the local Midland Bank Manager, Lay Reader and Church Treasurer, to consider the points raised by the doctor.

Quoting from the letter:

They desired me to point out that since the bells were fixed there have been only six peals in two years, one of which was for the Coronation. In 1950 eight bells hung in the tower but they were not often rung despite some of the funding coming from the Leicester Diocesan Association contributing in the hope that teams from other parishes would be allowed to ring at St Peter's.

'THE LETTER ENDED WITH A STING IN THE TALE'

.

The Rector mentioned this in his reply saying that applications to ring were often refused. He continued by pointing out: In other belfries bells were rung much more frequently so that your remark, 'the amount of bell ringing has been unreasonable', is wide of the mark, contrasted with other parishes.

The letter explained that bells were not rung when there were drama performances at St Peter's Hall and that Saturday afternoons between 4 PM and 7 PM for a peal seemed the best time to mitigate what a few regard as a public nuisance.

The Rector pointed out that peals were limited to one each quarter so that everything has been done to reduce annoyance to a minimum. Beyond that, he continued, I should not be prepared to go, even if I was staying in Bosworth. Those present were anxious to meet, as far as possible, any objection but the only practical suggestion was that you, and the hospital, shall have a fortnight's notice before a peal is rung. It is unfortunate that the hospital is in such close proximity to the church, but that is not the church's fault. The church and bells were there centuries before the hospital was thought of.

The letter ended with a sting in the tale for the recipient:

There is, however, a matter which you did not disclose in your letter to me and that is that you went into the church and interfered with the bell ropes and electric light. However annoyed you were there is no justification for such action. It might have caused a serious accident. Fortunately some candles were being used in the bell ringing chamber.

It is not known whether there was any further contact about the matter. The Rector, as hinted at in the letter, was about to leave Market Bosworth, he was at Bosworth from 1931 until 1954, to be replaced by William Edward Pilling, and Dr Kelly was later to retire to Ashby de la Zouch.

'ST GREGORY'S USED OUR CHURCH TO CELEBRATE MASS FOR THE FIRST TIME IN 500 YEARS'

Cyril Smith writes: At harvest festival time Orton on the Hill, Norton juxta Twycross and Austrey churches would stagger their services so that villagers could go to all three services on different Sundays. The churches looked a picture at these times with sheaves of corn placed around the lectern and the pulpits and fruit and vegetables on all the window sills. I can remember walking home on a brilliant moonlit night with the rest of the people from Norton. I had to go to church on my own in the morning, Sunday School in the afternoon and evening service with my mother. After the evening service, if the weather was nice, we would walk up Wood Lane to Gopsall, through a ride in the wood and have a look at the red deer and rare, black fallow deer in the Park.

Robert Leake writes: Our Lady and St Gregory's Roman Catholic Church was built in 1931. The church on Station Road was originally much smaller but extensions in 1975 and 1982 increased the capacity to accommodate 200 people. On September 6th 2009 Father Terry Fellows, with many of the congregation from St Gregory's in Market Bosworth, joined the congregation of St Peter's in a service to commemorate the 500th anniversary of the accession of Henry VIII. It was during Henry's reign that the split from Rome occurred which led to the foundation of the Church of England.

Diana Morgan writes: Last Sunday this congregation did something special that spoke volumes about who we are and what we value. We invited the Roman Catholic congregation of St Gregory's to use our church to celebrate Mass, for the first time in 500 years. We joined them and worshipped alongside them. It was John Plant, our Rector, who initially picked up the cross of Christian unity and issued the invitation to Father Terry. More of a challenge than an invitation was probably the thought of Father Terry because the structures and teachings of the Roman Catholic Church, particularly, make such a service very difficult but John and Father Terry addressed the problems as best they could and the service went ahead with St Peter's Church packed with Anglicans and Catholics. It was necessarily a compromise, a service that we enabled but couldn't fully partake in, but I think it would be hard not to have been moved and taken up by the sheer reverence of that Mass. I certainly felt very privileged to be there and it could be a first step to closer involvement.

Our Lady and St Gregory's Roman Catholic Church, Station Road

LEISURE

THE DICTIONARY DEFINITION OF 'LEISURE' IS 'FREE TIME' OR 'TIME AT ONE'S DISPOSAL THAT IS UNHURRIED'. LEISURE TIME TODAY IS OFTEN FULL OF ACTIVITY AND THE NEED TO BE GOING PLACES. BELOW ARE THE MEMORIES OF PEOPLE REMINISCING OF THE TIMES OF THEIR YOUTH, SOME SIXTY ODD YEARS AGO, WHEN LIFE SEEMED MUCH MORE RELAXED.

The contributors to this section were Fred Proudman, Philip Jenkins, Barbara Arm, Robert Taylor, Olive Hicklin, John Thorp and Blanche Symonds

Fred Proudman (in an extract from *Aspect* September 1973):

There was a night school for the youngsters and Canon Bowers had a room built at the Rectory where they could organize their own games. They organized a choir and a Drama Society which performed in the church school in Park Street. We had a Black and White Minstrel Show and they were very popular travelling around to local villages raising money for the church.

Philip Jenkins (in an extract from *Down Your Way – Brian Johnston's Radio Programme, 1976)*, talks of the Community Centre when he was Headmaster of the High School):

The Community Centre is based on the school and uses the school buildings. It runs evening classes and in fact day classes as well for adults. We are home to various affiliated societies and bodies, the Rugby Club uses our changing rooms, the Women's Institute come here for their meetings, the National Farmers' Union, the History Society, the Young Farmers' Club and all sorts of groups come here to use our centre.

Top: Rear view of the Old Rectory
Above: Black and White Minstrels

'SIR WOLSTAN DECIDED HE DIDN'T WANT LOCALS PLAYING THERE AT ALL'

Barbara Arm writes: The adults gave regular concerts; some of the inhabitants were really talented. I have a series of pictures, by Walter Shepherd, photographer, of a Flea Circus that came to Bosworth.

Blanche Symonds writes: I played for the Ladies' Cricket Team where I met Richard, better known as Dick, who was also a keen cricketer. The original cricket pitch was on Bosworth Estate land between The Park and Cadeby Lane. It became overgrown and the Club moved to the Bosworth Showground land but eventually Sir Wolstan Dixie wanted the pitch back on its original site. Time was spent preparing the ground and on Sundays professional players from Leicester held their matches there; then Sir Wolstan decided he didn't want locals playing there at all. As the Showground pitch was in a poor state the Cricket Club folded until the new pitch off Wellsborough Road was created.

John Thorp – I remember going to watch the local football team play in their team colours of black and amber. Charlie Stanton used to bring the tea at half time in a big urn and Harry March was the linesman. I remember Harry March telling me that when he was a lad he used to go to Ibstock and once he got threatened by a chap who said he was a champion boxer. Harry said to him, 'I'm a champion runner so you'll have to catch me first'.

In winter time we used to go sledging on Silk Hill, I have painful memories of going down there and hitting the gatepost. Then we would skate on the canal. I just recently sold the ice skates that I used. I remember a car being driven on the frozen canal and Bob Ryley was known to have skated from Hinckley to Bosworth when the canal was frozen.

On Saturday nights we went dancing at the Coalville Grande. There were more local dances in those days; the Young Farmers had dances, they used to have local beauty queen dances in aid of the Hunt. We went to a lot of Whist Drives and there used to be a cinema at the NATSOPA Home, Wellsborough and at the Nurses' Home where we would go to watch films.

Top: Walter Shepherd
Above: Mr W H Beck with Charlie Stanton (right)

'BEST FIELD I'VE EVER PLAYED ON, NEVER HAD MUD ON MY BOOTS NO MATTER WHAT THE WEATHER.'

Bob Taylor (landlord of the Red Lion Hotel from 1964 to 1984) — A crowd of us used to go to the local keep fit class once a week at the gym and at the end of the season it was decided that as we were getting fitter we ought to play rugger again. We played on the school field for a start and then rented a field on Cadeby Lane from Mr Hodgetts at the Hall, best field I've ever played on, never had mud on my boots no matter what the weather. He wouldn't sell that one when they wanted to buy a field so they bought the one next to it, it sloped a bit but it's alright. They used the showers at the school and then they used to come back to our place, go in the club room and have food and whatnot up there and so it started all very small but jocular. That was good fun for a couple of years when we only had one or two teams but then it got too big. They started to build their own club house on the ground they have now and it went from strength to strength. They now have a mini-rugby team and they have hundreds of kids there on a Sunday morning.

Tommy Dixon was a racing driver from Perth in Scotland; he and his mechanics used to stay for bed and breakfast. They had been racing at Silverstone a week before and were going on to Mallory Park. Tommy had a racing car on a trailer and his mechanics had changed the gearbox but they hadn't had chance to test it, so he said, 'I should like to test it before I go up to the track. Is there anywhere quiet I can go because, obviously, it's not road taxed?' I told him that he could go straight down through Carlton and Barton as far as Snarestone then turn round and come right back. He was not too sure of the directions and asked, 'Do you want to come with me and show me the way?' I asked him what time he was going. About four or five in the morning was the reply. It was summer time and light in the morning so I said all right. We got this flipping thing off the trailer, but it wouldn't start so he did no more than take all the plugs out, replace them and then off we went. Park Street was a two-way road at that time and he was sitting at the end of the road revving it up; the noise would have bounced around the Square because there was no silencer on it, and off we shot.

'IT WAS THE QUICKEST TRIP I'VE EVER HAD TO SNARESTONE AND BACK IN MY LIFE'

He had a helmet and visor on but he hadn't got a spare and, with the windscreen being about three inches high, every time I looked up my eyes filled with water, I couldn't see a thing. It was the quickest trip I've ever had to Snarestone and back in my life, and the most hilarious; I didn't really feel frightened because, obviously, he could drive the thing. After you go through Barton there is a really sharp bend, we went round the second bit and there was an old Morris Minor coming the other way - I don't know how we missed it but it must have frightened the driver to death! He used to drive for Ecurie Ecosse, the Scottish team.

'THERE WAS AN OLD MORRIS MINOR COMING THE OTHER WAY - I DON'T KNOW HOW WE MISSED IT'

Olive Hicklin –When we lived at Congerstone we had a lovely childhood. During the holidays, Mum would make us some lemonade and she would fill two big bottles with tea. With these drinks and some sandwiches off we went across the fields. We decided not to play with the other village children because we learnt that if we went with other children and something happened we would get the blame and the strap. So we played on our own. We always went to the water where there were wild raspberries and wild crab apples and watercress. My dad used to say, 'Now don't pull up the roots of the watercress and give it a wash because of the little black beetles.'

I must have eaten millions of them! We would take off our shoes and socks and get the baby out of the pram. We never saw any danger and we would be out all day until we started to feel hungry so then we went home for our tea, although we always had to wait for my dad to come home so that we could all sit round the table together.

We used to have a maypole on May Day. We would go round the village with a basket to each house to ask for some flowers for the maypole. We also went and collected cowslips and may-blobs (*marsh marigold*) and then in the evening we would tip them all out on this big table and we would all help to make little bunches. My dad placed them all round this big hoop and sprinkled them with water for the night. The biggest boy carried the maypole and we always had a May Queen. I was never the May Queen because the dress didn't fit me! Lucy was May Queen for two years, I was maid of honour. Miss Rolleston, at the Rectory, kept the dresses and dressed the May Queen. We went round first thing in the morning before school and went singing, carrying the Red Cross collecting tin. After school we would get dressed up again and we would walk as far as Bilstone with the tin. My dad made the maypole every year.

TRADE, INDUSTRY AND TRANSPORT

MARKET BOSWORTH CONTINUES TO BE A THRIVING MARKET TOWN WITH MANY LOCAL COMPANIES AND TRADESMEN PROVIDING A WIDE RANGE OF GOODS AND SERVICES TO LOCAL RESIDENTS AND VISITORS ALIKE. THE MEMORIES CAPTURED BELOW ARE TESTAMENT TO THE ROLE OF THE TOWN AS AN IMPORTANT COMMERCIAL CENTRE FOR THE SURROUNDING RURAL HINTERLAND

Contributors to this section were Barbara Arm, Olive Hicklin, Brian Oakley, Robert Jarvis, Robert Taylor, Susan Andrews, Kay Palmer and an extract from Down Your Way 1976 with Colin Lowe.

Barbara Arm writes: At eight months old I went to live at Market Bosworth at the Red Lion Hotel. Whilst living there my grandfather had a small brewery where beer was brewed for the Hotel. The hops were fetched from Bosworth Station. The brew house had three rooms in which there were big coppers. Whilst we lived at the Red Lion my uncles came every day to brew the beer which was then delivered to various farms round the district. Also the mail was taken from the Red Lion, Market Bosworth, to Nuneaton. The Royal Mail was driven by horses, again by my uncles. I don't know how long that continued.

Olive Hicklin — My father worked all over the place. He did a lot of work at Prestwold Hall,

Loughborough, and used to have to find lodgings when he worked there. He also worked at Gopsall Hall. Opposite the school at Congerstone was a great big tree which my dad had to fell. The teacher, Miss Ethall, who was lovely, wanted the school children to see this big tree being felled. I will never forget it. The teacher thanked my dad for letting the children watch. In the summer my father would get jobs with farmers often cutting hedges. He always had jobs to go to and they would last him through the summer months when they couldn't fell the trees. One day, my father got permission for us to go in the grounds of Gopsall Hall so we could see the deer. There was this gorgeous lake with a lovely boathouse and a landing stage. We saw the deer and I remember all the trees with lovely deep red blossom.

Deer, Gopsall Park

'THE MILL WAS BUILT IN CARLTON STONE AND WAS MENTIONED IN THE DOMESDAY BOOK'

There was a dump down at the railway station. The soldiers had a petrol dump down there during World War II and after they had gone it was made into a tip. The Council had the tip as a sort of salvage place and Madge and I asked my dad if we could work there if we did all the jobs at home in the morning and the washing at night. Mum was quite ill so we had a job persuading my dad to let us go and work down there. Well we went to the Council Offices and we both got a job. We stayed down on the dump. There were a lot of girls who used to go out collecting salvage but we didn't go. I stayed working at the dump until I was about sixteen and a half and then my mum took really bad again. We used to do the washing on a Monday night and she used to come in and ask if she could help. I think it mithered her to death to see us doing it because we had been working all day. We used to say to her, 'Go and put the kettle on, Mum', and then we used to have this Camp coffee. We managed because she was at home to look after the kiddies but we did all the work. Then she took even worse and I couldn't go to work any more and Madge got married.

Brian Oakley – When I was a boy I helped Mr Bill Drackley, the miller. Mr Drackley was a very big, strong man but talked softly and was a gentle chap. The Mill was down a separate track from the house and it had a stable type door on it. The Mill was built in stone; I can remember that, Carlton stone. They say it was mentioned in the Domesday Book so it's pretty old. The entrance to it was just a stable door. As you looked inside, it always seemed very gloomy because there was no electric there of course. There was on the left hand side, I think, a paraffin motor, then if the water ran out you could always start up the motor to

take over the turning of the stone. When you got inside - all dust and cobwebs, a lot of woodwork, a lot of beams and a lot of hoppers all interesting - there was a set of granary steps where you went up to the first floor.

Left Bosworth Mill, Barton Road
Above: Mr Bill Drackley, the miller

NATSOPA – THE NATIONAL SOCIETY OF OPERATIVE PRINTERS AND ASSISTANTS

The millstones were on the first floor and these had to be dressed regularly. A pulley system was used to raise them for dressing. The gears were constructed of timber, probably oak, and these had to be changed fairly often. Beck's Builders would maintain these. Beck's also serviced the paddles on the waterwheel. Whoever did this job got a 1d or 1½d extra an hour as it was not a pleasant task. The mill-pond ran from the main road up to the Mill and this was fed from the Stoney Brook via a manmade channel, regulated by a sluice gate in a field where the Woods farmed. From the mill-pond down to the Stoney Brook there was a lovely set of brick steps for the overflow.

I was about ten when I started at the Mill as a spare time job which was some nights and all day on a Saturday. My main job was to watch the bags that were filling up with the flour so they didn't overfill. Some of the hoppers you had to fill by hand with a wooden shovel. The hessian sacks went onto four hooks so it was open at the top.

Jobs taken on at a young age could lead to full-time employment.

Robert Jarvis – My father, Arch Jarvis, started his working life as a gardener: He started at Bosworth Hall

NATSOPA MEMORIAL HOMES

when he was a young lad. During the war he was in the Home Guard, after that he moved to the National Printers' Convalescent Home where he was taken on as Head Gardener and had eight to ten people working with him. Quite a few local people worked up there, at that time of day, and produced all the vegetables, fruit and eggs that were needed. They reared pigs and turkeys and things at Christmas; it was a self-sufficient convalescent home. People would come from the Printers' Union in London to convalesce, most with respiratory problems; there was a hospital, cinema and chapel there. There was a little shop and everything on site for them. They had their own little rooms and houses. Some people retired there and they had bungalows that they lived in until the actual Memorial Homes were turned over to the Holy Ghost Fathers, as they were called then; they were a priesthood. My father stayed for a little while after that but he was 68 at the time and he decided it wasn't the job for him because he found that the young monks didn't want the labour, they wanted the easy jobs. You could see that the place was going into disrepair and getting run down so he decided to give it up but he did fifty three years there before he retired.

Aerial view of the NATSOPA Memorial Homes, Wellsborough

'EVERY FLOOR ON THE LONDON UNDERGROUND SYSTEM HAS BEEN TREATED BY US'

There was a strong family tradition in some local firms. One such example was the Timber Fireproofing Company Limited located off Station Road.

Colin Lowe (Chief Executive of the Timber Fireproofing Company Ltd in a *'Down Your Way'* interview in 1976): We employ some forty odd people and have a lot of inter-related people working within the establishment, brothers, fathers and sons, this sort of situation. Another interesting point about this is that we seem to have very little turnover of working people, the shortest time basis on the place, at the moment, is some seven or eight years.

It's been here something in the region of forty years. The reason for them coming to Market Bosworth was that one of the old directors of the company, when it was a private company, happened to own land in Bosworth. Because of the situation with the site, with the canal on one side and the railway on the other, these being the means of transport some forty years ago, it was an ideal situation for the operation.

The aim and object is to render timber and timber type products such as plywood, hardboard, chipboard, cork, resistant to fire. We restrict the combustion of the material and this gives people sufficient time to get out of a fire situation and therefore saves their life. We place the timber or the plywood into pressure vessels and flood a fire retardant chemical into the cylinders, Many thousands of people everyday use the London Underground system and every floor that they walk on has been treated by us. We have done timbers for the British Aircraft Corporation and Aerospatiale and there is a quantity of treated timber being used on Concorde.

Timber Fireproofing Co Ltd, Station Road

'WE WORKED SEVEN DAYS A WEEK WHEN I FIRST STARTED, FOR A SMALL AMOUNT OF MONEY'

Many changes have been seen over the years in the way business is conducted. Local trades were learned on the job from experienced professionals, supplemented by college courses. Robert Jarvis recollects that he was told he had got a job in the butchers when he left school. His father, being a friend of Mr Lampard Snr had already organised for him to start work. So he left school one week and started work the next. He wanted to go into commercial art; design, graphic printing and that sort of thing but he never did and he started work in the butchers and has stayed there ever since. He has thoroughly enjoyed meeting people and really watching Bosworth grow.

Robert Jarvis — There has been a tremendous amount of change in butchery in my life, since I started there. Basically we worked seven days a week when I first started working and for a small amount of money. Mondays we worked half a day and the rest of the week was preparing, cutting meat, making sausage and boning bacon. I didn't work in the shop for at least three or four years as there was one person who ran the shop; Bosworth wasn't very large at that time. He managed the shop on his own and looked after that and worked at the rear of the shop. We had two vans on the road which delivered around the villages. In 1966 the shop was re-developed as Mr Lampard Jnr could see that Bosworth was going to grow with the Springfield Estate being built. He decided we

needed a larger shop which was done and opened up six months later. After that we started to employ more staff because, in the beginning there was only Mr Bill Lampard himself, Jim Lampard and a fellow called Dick Turner. They were the only people who worked there at that time but once the shop developed and things started to grow, they employed youngsters from school. Then we started delivering more and more and had three vans on the road. Mr Lampard Snr was still alive at that time and was doing a van round three days a week until he was seventy five. When he retired I took over the rounds that he did.

Through Mr Lampard Snr I went to Leicester College to do a course in biology. I learnt more about the make-up of meat, diseases and problems that animals get. We went to the cattle market to look at the offal and were given a test, that was part and parcel. Also we would go to different shops in the city to cut meat up in front of our teachers, the examiners, and set a window up or a counter so they could see how we were improving with what we were doing.

Above: Lampard's slaughter yard
Right: Lampard's delivery vans

'SHE WAS TAKEN DOWN TO THE GAS WORKS TO SMELL THE GAS WHEN SHE HAD WHOOPING-COUGH'

Barbara Arm writes: The Gas Works at Market Bosworth was in Station Road. The lighting in the bigger houses in Bosworth was all by gas but in the 1920s the Gas Works closed down and people had to have oil lamps again. My mother could remember being taken down to the Gas Works at Bosworth to smell the gas when she had whooping-cough because it was supposed to be very good for them. The Hinckley Electric Company brought electricity to Bosworth in 1931 or 1932.

Robert Taylor – Hoskins Brewery bought the Red Lion Hotel just before the war and the reason they did it was because they had many off-licence sales. To have an outside event you had to have a Publican's Licence and Market Bosworth Show was the big one. We were unique, especially when CAMRA (Campaign for Real Ale) got on the bandwagon; they used to come from far and wide. The wife and I took over in around about 1962/1963.

When my dad was there (*he took over as landlord of the Red Lion in 1954*), he had petrol pumps as well, one either side of the car park entrance, but he gave that up because the local garage sold petrol. On the top, where they park now, there was a garage. It was a garage-cum-stable; there were two big sliding doors; they had got a drainage piece at the back and also rings all along the wall where they obviously used to tie the horses when they were there; probably been there since the 1800s.

Right: Gas Works, Station Road
Left: Park Street, showing petrol pumps

'THERE WAS A LOAD OF THEM DRINKING HOSKINS LIKE THERE WAS NO TOMORROW'

A lot of the locals, to be honest, didn't like Hoskins beer which was a real ale. So at one time I sold more draught Guinness than anybody in the county I think. Then one Saturday lunchtime a crowd of guys came in, had the Hoskins, oh, they loved it, smashing! They said they had got to go to a meeting in Nuneaton in the afternoon and that's when they formed CAMRA. I saw something written where it was formed in Wales, or somewhere, but it wasn't, take it from me, it was formed in Nuneaton because they came back on the Sunday morning and till 2 PM there was a load of them drinking Hoskins like there was no tomorrow. They were all from the Manchester area.

'BUT THEN SUDDENLY THESE GUYS

GOT IT BY THE SCRUFF OF THE

NECK'

The hardcore ones that formed CAMRA were quite knowledgeable. It was like any of these societies, a lot of people jump on the bandwagon because they go round with flags flying, funny hats on. It did a good thing actually because when they formed CAMRA you had a job to find any real ale like ours because then it was all Watneys Red Barrel, and Double Diamond keg beer. Keg beers were taking over completely. I think the Black Horse had Double Diamond, the sale of real ale was going out the window, but then suddenly these guys got it by the scruff of the neck and I think it's as strong now as it's ever been. Most pubs nowadays you can go in and get guest draught beers where you couldn't at one time. The trouble is real ale takes a bit of keeping; because of the way it's pumped air keeps getting in which has to be vented otherwise its shelf life deteriorates. With keg beer nothing can get in so it is much easier to keep.

We had Hoskins bitter and Hoskins mild but that was all. One of the Hoskins' family went to the Royal Show and came back and said, 'I have tasted something there and it's quite good'. It was Carlsberg Export Lager. Nobody sold lager and anyway he said, 'I think we're going to try it', and they did and it was a nice drink.

We still sold Guinness and one day one of the reps came in and he said, 'Mr Taylor, we'll have to come and change your Guinness'. I said what do you mean change the Guinness? 'Well,' he said, 'it's got to go through a cooler now.' I said a cooler? It's perfect as it is; it's come up out the cellar. He said, 'Oh no, you have got to have a cooler.' I said well, you can take the Guinness out then - all blasé. But to be fair to them, they had stopped brewing the old sort. They had brewed it to go through a cooler but at the time I couldn't see the reason for the change.

'I THOUGHT RUGBY PLAYERS CAN DRINK BUT MUSICIANS ARE A CLOSE SECOND I CAN TELL YOU'

I used to like a bottle of Guinness myself; the old style Guinness, but you couldn't get a decent bottle

anywhere. One day when I was working down at the Cock at Sibson we had a crowd of Guinness reps in at lunchtime. I said by the way while you are here why can't you get a decent bottle of Guinness? 'You can.' I said you can't, the stuff in the supermarket is not the same as it used to be. They looked at each other and grinned and they told me that it's all pasteurised now. Whereas there used to be living yeast or whatnot in the bottle, you didn't pour a Guinness right out like you can now, it keeps better. The old bottle of Guinness, I think, only had a shelf life of about three or four weeks to be really top notch.

The CAMRA thing flourished till after I left. We used to have bus loads come and all sorts. We had a minibus load of chaps came in one lunchtime, ordered some drinks and, as we didn't do food at the time, they asked if they could go up to the butchers and get some pork pie and rolls so that they could eat. While they were gone a big van came round with Royal Philharmonic Orchestra on the side and that pulled in the car park and they came in. I thought rugby players can drink but musicians are a close second I can tell you, and they had got to do a rehearsal in Nottingham in the afternoon and a concert at night. They were very interesting. Some of the people you got in came from all walks of life; Bill Maynard often came in.

Hoskins Brewery sold up and a wine firm bought it but Hoskins wouldn't sell the pub on its own, they wanted it to go as a job lot so the wine growers bought it. They said we would be alright but the day they took over they gave us six months notice.

Cock Inn, Sibson

'NOT MANY OF THE FAMILIES LIVING IN BOSWORTH AT THAT TIME
POSSESSED PRIVATE TRANSPORT'

Susan Andrews – I was born at the King William IV public house in 1948 but later moved to the Park and then back to the King William lV. In 1940 my maternal grandparents took over the King William IV public house in Market Bosworth and Mum came to live with them. In the meantime the Hinckley and Bosworth Borough Council were building prefabs, these were prefabricated houses and they were built in the vicinity of Southfield Way. They were put up because of the war and it was a quick way of getting people into houses. My mother was told that she would be entitled to one of these, but she gave up her rights to the prefab as her brother and his wife had no where to live.

Life in the early fifties was very free and easy and quiet as very little traffic passed through Bosworth and not many of the families living in Bosworth at that time possessed private transport.

My earliest memories are mostly of the pub life at that time. Being an only child it was quite lonely being upstairs in the flat above the pub on your own and sometimes I would go down and sit behind the bar on a beer crate and watch Mum and Dad and listen to the conversations going on.

People that used to come into the pub, especially the Smoke Room, were Bert Williamson, the butcher, David Salmon and Geoff Brown, the insurance man. They used to be regulars everyday in the Smoke Room, they would come and hold forth. The Cheshire brothers - Norman, Horace, Joe and Cyril - and Jimmy Lively, used to frequent the Bar. They formed the nucleus of the darts team; a very good darts team.

Darts team, King William IV

'HE WOULD LINE THEM UP ON THE BAR AND EACH PINT GLASS WOULD HAVE THEIR NAME WRITTEN ON IT IN GOLD PAINT'

I remember Sunday mornings at the pub particularly because every Sunday at midday all the regulars would be knocking on the door to the Bar. On the dot of 12 noon Dad would open up and let everyone in, but before he did that he would pour everybody a pint. As they were regulars he knew exactly what they wanted and he would line them up on the bar and each pint glass would have their name written on it in gold paint. This ritual went on for many years. The King Bill was known for its regulars, some of them you could set your clock by. The pub in those days acted as a meeting place and being such a small village everybody knew everybody else.

I remember the winters in the fifties were proper winters and you would have inches of snow every year. We would long for it to get really deep so we could go sledging down Silk Hill, which as kids was great fun. We would all run down the Back Lane past the slaughter house and into the field, across the field and up Silk Hill. All the fields and Silk Hill belonged to Hollier's farm.

I remember wonderful summer holidays playing tennis with my dad on Hollier's tennis court. He was quite a good tennis player and was always pressured to take part in a game or two, usually on a Sunday because the pub opening hours were much shorter than in the week. We were open from midday until 2 PM and then opened again at 7 PM and closed at 10 PM. Trevor Jones, the sergeant, and a police constable would look into the bar just before 10 PM and ask dad if everything was okay before moving on to the next pub.

I remember riding Shirley Hollier's ponies, Robin and Ginny, with Shirley in the fields round the slaughter house and Silk Hill. We always came home having been thrown off the pony in a hedge or two, with cuts and bruises but we didn't seem to mind, just went back for some more. One of the things we used to do in the summer holidays was take pop and crisps and go to the Stoney Brook. We were out all day, nobody bothered us. In the fifties the brook was quite visible and you got to it across an open field. You would run in and out of the brook getting quite wet and dirty, sit and eat whatever you had brought with you and run back home at the end of the day. We never got into any trouble and no harm came to us.

King William IV sign

'MY MOTHER, CISSIE GLYDE, WORKED AT CHURCHILL'S MAKING BULLETS ON THE NIGHT SHIFT, 8 TILL 8'

During the war my mother, Cissie Glyde, worked at Churchill's in Bosworth making bullets on the night shift, 8 till 8, after that she helped my dad in the pub. She also did volunteer work in the Red Cross shop which was situated in one of the wooden Wembley houses next to where the garage was. My mum and dad met on the Monkey Walk in Swadlincote; so called because at night after work and school, people would come out of their houses and walk up and down and chat together. In the thirties there wasn't a lot of entertainment.

'THERE WAS SO MUCH FREEDOM AND

SPACE WHICH IS SOMETHING TODAY'S

CHILDREN WILL NEVER BE ABLE TO

EXPERIENCE'

The work of a pub in those days didn't give Mum and Dad much time for socialising as you were open seven days a week and only closed on Christmas Day. They didn't have any help and all the cleaning, decorating and the everyday running of the pub Mum and Dad did between them. I do remember that on Show Day it was like an invasion. Mum and Dad had to get help in on Show Day in the pub. We had to get in extra beer, wine and spirits because we knew we would sell them. The crates were stacked up outside. It was just bedlam from morn till night. For a kid of about seven or eight it was great to be running about

in and out of the pub because there was always something going on. It was the one day in the year that Mum and Dad had help.
Hetty Granger and her husband, Roland, would be enlisted to help on that day. Hetty would wash the glasses and Roland would collect empty glasses and take empty bottles et cetera outside, while Mum and Dad would stand practically all day, it seemed, serving customers.

I remember the Cattle Market and listening to the auctioneer, and being able to run up and down the lines of pens patting the livestock; sheep, pigs whatever there was.

We played marbles and used the hula hoop in the play ground at the Junior School in Bosworth and played hop scotch and snobs. I suppose looking back I had an idyllic childhood; there was so much freedom and space, which is something today's children will never be able to experience.

King William IV 1966

'ONE COULD BE USED AS A BUS, ANOTHER WAS A FLAT BODY AND ANOTHER
 WAS A HEARSE'

Barbara Arm writes: At the Dixie Arms
Hotel in Market Bosworth the
tenant was Walter Shepherd who
was also a local photographer and
there are many cards around from
his collection. He was the maker
of the Tin Lizzie Ford, the parts
of which were sent from the
American Ford Motor Company.
They were assembled at the back
of the Dixie Arms. Altogether he
had seven different bodies to the
Tin Lizzie Ford, mostly made of
wood and tin and then put on the
Ford Chassis. One could be used
as a bus, another was a flat body
and another was a hearse.

The first person to buy the bus
body was a Mr Morton of
Nuneaton. He used it to take the
miners to work, come back and
reload with girls to take to the
factories. This body was the
forerunner of the buses.

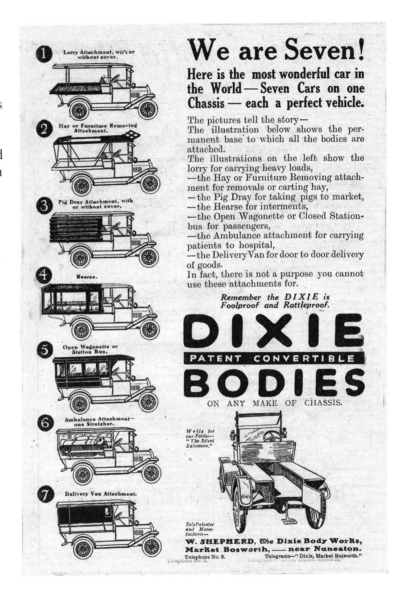

'ON WEDNESDAYS HE CONVERTED IT INTO A LORRY TO TRANSPORT SHEEP OR CALVES TO LEICESTER MARKET'

My uncle, Mr Harry Trivett, who lived at the Red Lion, purchased one in 1919 for £350. He used it as a twelve seater bus and charged a shilling return to Leicester on Saturdays. Then on Wednesdays he

converted it into a lorry to transport sheep or calves to Leicester market. He also collected orders for groceries and various items from shops and libraries. They would send the orders down to the cloakroom of the Hare and Pheasant in High Street, Leicester to be brought back to Market Bosworth. The tyres on this transport were solid, making the ride very rough, especially as the roads were also very rough. Mr W H Trivett also had a brake, a type of horse drawn bus drawn by two horses abreast, within which people sat face to face. This was used mostly for outings and transporting football teams.

Kay Palmer writes: There was a police sergeant and a constable living in the village and we saw them around and respected them. They kept law and order quite well. I was friends with the sergeant's daughter and spent lots of time in the sergeant's house. There was also a constable's house which was pulled down and the magistrate's courtrooms are now the arts centre for the Grammar School. There were one or two cells at the back of the courtrooms where people awaiting trial were kept. Mr Brown, for whom my grandmother was housekeeper for, was a magistrate. It was minor cases that were dealt with but it was a disgrace, of course, to go before them. There was not much vandalism in Bosworth because the police would see to that and they were backed up by the parents because if the police went to your parents, you got into trouble from them as well.

My father worked at Beale's shop and when I was eight or nine Mr Beale retired and we took over the shop which was then known as D G Quincey's. We sold groceries, wines and spirits, seeds and chemist items. Everything we sold had to be weighed or measured. Sugar came in sacks, tea in silver-paper lined chests; my father had his own blend of tea to suit the local water. Butter came in half hundredweight blocks, to be cut and weighed. Dried fruit came in 56lb sacks to be weighed out and wrapped in special blue paper. Figs arrived in 14lb hessian bags, vinegar in barrels and tarragon port in quart bottles, to be sold at 3/6d.

One of the Dixie bodies

FARMING

MARKET BOSWORTH IS AT THE CENTRE OF A LARGELY AGRICULTURAL AREA. FARMING IS STILL AN IMPORTANT INDUSTRY BUT THERE ARE NOW FEWER BUT GENERALLY LARGER FARMS. FARMING AT ONE TIME OFFERED EMPLOYMENT TO THE MAJORITY OF THE LOCAL WORKING POPULATION. MIXED FARMING WAS WIDESPREAD BUT TODAY FARMS TEND TO SPECIALISE AND FOCUS ON ONE ASPECT OF THE INDUSTRY.

Contributors to this section were Gordon and Jill Earp from Osbaston House Farm, Joy Crane from Temple Hall Farm, Wellsborough, Patrick Green from Westfield Farm and, later, Lower and Upper Coton Farm and Alan Eames from Hall Farm, Osbaston

Patrick Green – In the late 1920s my father, Leslie Lovell Green, together with other like-minded business and professional friends, formed a Back to the Land Movement and to pursue its aims bought Westfield Farm on the Congerstone Road west of Bosworth. It was managed by the Midland Catholic Land Association and its aim was to take unemployed Catholic men from industrial districts and train them in all branches of husbandry. They would then be established on their own land with approximately 30-35 acres, given farming tackle with a view to providing a living for a man and his family. Forty men were trained, and taught most of the branches of mixed farming, but because the Association had been unable to get Government funding the project closed after running for approximately three years.

The farm consisted of 188 acres; some of which were used for growing oats, wheat and potatoes. In time, some of the acreage was given over to barley, vegetables and root crops and some let out for grazing.

Father Francis Tierney was the chaplain and warden of the farm and lived in the farmhouse with some of the trainees; the others being accommodated at Westfield's other four cottages. Mass was celebrated each day in a ground-floor room converted into a chapel.

'ITS AIM WAS TO TAKE UNEMPLOYED

CATHOLIC MEN FROM INDUSTRIAL

DISTRICTS'

The idea of working all day for as little pay as they might expect on the dole did not appeal to any but the most idealistic. The project was not a long term success. However, my father's interest in farming increased and in the early 1930s he bought Upper Far Coton Farm which was tenanted. Later, in the 1940s, the tenant gave up and the farm was managed thereafter with my father and, later, myself having direct control of farming activities.

Westfield Farm

'MY FATHER BOUGHT A BULL CALF AT MARKET AND IT TRAVELLED ON
THE BACK SEAT OF THEIR LITTLE VAUXHALL 12'

We still used horses for carting and ploughing
in the thirties but during the war we started to
use tractors and I learnt to drive an old
Fordson when about twelve years old in 1943.
The corn was stacked in the field after drying
in stooks and was always beautifully thatched.
In September or October the thrashing
machine would arrive with the steam-driven
traction engine. Then the corn was carted
again back to the farmyard. I was not allowed
to drive on the road. Afterwards we would
have a harvest supper and there could be up to
thirty people attending – this for a farm of
about 300 acres – mixed corn, sheep, pigs,
hens, turkeys and dairy cows.

By the 1950s my father had bought Lower
Far Coton Farm, originally owned by
Mrs Shepherd and run by her son-in-law,
Mr Thirlby. Mrs Thirlby was related to
Michael Colin Cowdrey the England cricketer.
He visited them and together we used to go

shooting, mainly pigeons, in our two large
woods. Later still, Lower Farm was managed
as one with Upper Farm. In those days we
were mainly self-sufficient and Mr Bert
Williamson, our manager, made sausages.
Later he left and opened a butcher's shop in
Market Bosworth Square.

Early on in the days of building a herd of
pedigree Ayrshires (1950s) my father bought a
bull calf at market and it travelled on the back
seat of our little car, a Vauxhall 12. He must
have hit a pothole because he broke a rear
spring on the way back. This pedigree calf was
of the Minstead dynasty and he was given the
name Minstead Mainspring after that.

Above: Taking the harvest home
Left: Upper Far Coton Farm

'THERE WAS NO ELECTRICITY UNTIL 1936 WHEN MY FATHER PAID FOR A CONNECTION FROM THE TOLLGATE'

Gordon Earp – There was no electricity until 1936 when my father paid for a connection from the Tollgate. Prior to this oil lamps were the only source of light in the house and in the cow sheds where milking was done by hand. Milk was then emptied into old-fashioned coolers; the water being pumped by wind power into a reservoir at the front of the house. The milk was taken to Bosworth Station early each morning and delivered eventually to Express Dairies in London. About thirty cows were milked by hand until the advent of machines when electricity was installed. Also in the 1930s the farm had its first tractor, a Fordson, and a Ford 8 car. Together they cost just over £200. I drove the tractor from about the age of eleven.

Threshing was always contracted out and initially we had a bloke named Swifty Statham, they used to be at Newbold, they were a bit 'come day go day, God send Sunday', like you didn't know when they would turn up. Later we had Hentons from Norton, we were always pleased to see them come and always pleased to see them go. It was hard work in those days. The old threshing engines used to work on coal and water and you had to have a lot of coal to work them. We had to get up at about 6 AM to get the damper off to get the steam up ready to start. The grain was stored in eighteen stone sacks in those days and they were carted up the ladder to the loft on the workers' backs. The wheat went largely to Minions Wharf at Atherstone.

A Marshall threshing machine at Bilstone

'HIS TOMATOES WERE SPECIALLY FED FROM THE LIQUID PRODUCED BY SOAKING THE SHEEP DAGENDS IN WATER'

Joy Greenfield lived at Temple Hall Farm, Wellsborough, from when she was eight years old. She moved there from a farm in Lincolnshire with her mother and father and five brothers, in April 1949. On being asked if she had been spoilt her immediate answer was, 'I wasn't, they were'.

Joy Greenfield – The farm was Crown property and initially consisted of 300 acres, with approximately 50 dairy cows, plus pigs, sheep and, of course, poultry. My father liked to keep a Jersey cow so that he could have homemade butter which my mother made weekly and I can remember occasionally having to stand churning the barrel. My father's main interest was breeding Essex and Landrace pigs which he sold in spring at auctions held at the farm; people came from all over the country to the renowned annual pig sale. It took ages to prepare for it, all the pigs had to be numbered and their family history written down. This was my job and, before the sale, the men took over and washed and combed them. It was also a very busy time in the kitchen because half the folks would want a meal if they had bought any animals. I, of course, had to help prepare the food.

Harry Greenfield was also well-known for his tomatoes, specially fed from the liquid produced by soaking the sheep dagends in water which made a very good fertiliser. *(Dagends - the clippings taken from around a sheep's backside before it was introduced to the tup or ram).*

I was an active member of the local Young Farmers and remember the time when Mrs Pearce from the Black Horse was unable to prepare the Harvest Supper and I, when fifteen, volunteered to help and, of course, ended up doing all the catering.

Temple Hall Farm, Wellsborough

'WELLSBOROUGH ILLUMINATIONS'

The Christmas Fatstock was the highlight of the year as the Young Farmers had their own Calf Club. After rearing their calves throughout the year the competition was on to see who had the best calf in the Show. At various times I won and so did my brothers.

I remember the time when the farm was troubled by foxes taking the new born lambs that were held in the field at the front of the farm. Bill Wykes of Sibson fixed up lights round the field to keep the foxes at bay. It worked, and there was much talk of the Wellsborough Illuminations amongst the locals.

Mr Greenfield liked to show off his garden so in the summer there would always be several events planned like the Free Church Garden Fête, trips organised by the local council and also NFU farm walks. The farm was used as a community facility.

Joy ended her interview by saying it had made her realise how busy they all were but they were never bored: We didn't have a lot of money to spend on expensive toys and entertainment but we never, ever had an idle moment.

Jill Earp (whose family farmed at Thurlaston) – As a four year-old I had a cade lamb, an orphan, which adopted me as Mum and followed me for about a mile into the village where I was in a festival dressed as Mary had a little lamb.

Alan Eames (whose family farmed Hall Farm, Osbaston) writes: It was like most medium sized farms of that size in the '50s because the day of the combine harvester had not fully arrived.

Instead we would use schemes and machinery not so very different from those a hundred years before. The only real change was the use of the tractor instead of the heavy horse. After the previous harvest the field would be scuffled, ploughed and disked in the autumn to make a nice even tilth and then, depending on the crop, fertilised and sown. Often we would use manure from the cattle and pigs and poultry before ploughing in but sometimes artificial fertiliser would be spread.

Top: Jill Earp with cade lamb
Above left: Hall Farm, Osbaston

'KING'S CLOSE, TOWNSEND, BROAD MEADOW, FOLFORDS'

Mercury seed dressings were also common to prevent the ravages of parasites and I remember mixing these in. We were also pretty happy to use sprays! But my dad was also careful to organise a good crop rotation so the diseases of one year could not carry over to a similar crop.

The fields all had names; Kings Close, Townsend, Broad Meadow, Folfords. The crop was winter wheat, spring barley, or oats. Usually no problems till harvest time came

round then it was a question of the weather, or if you were really unlucky, a cereal disease might strike. I remember my father almost in tears looking at a crop affected by the 'take-all' fungus, well named because it took all, and there was hardly any seed in the ears of corn.

On a good dry day we would get the binder out. Making the binder ready involved finding the canvases, mending the straps and sharpening the knives which were driven off a big wheel as the machine was pulled along, originally by horses, but in my day by the tractor. We had three tractors, one an antiquated Fordson with metal spiked wheels which was rarely used and two red Case

machines; all ran on a petrol start and paraffin main fuel. All had to be swung with the handle to start, none had batteries, the spark plugs were fed by a magneto; they made a great clatter.

Someone not very important had to sit on the binder and watch to make sure all was well. If you dozed or were thinking of other things you could be in bad trouble, suddenly realising there were a hundred untied sheaves lying in a row behind. The field corners had already been cleared by a man with a scythe; a tool used for hundreds of years before the coming of machines, and you tied up those sheaves with a twist of the corn stalk itself.

The last bit of the crop in the middle of the field was exciting because in here would be hiding all the birds and animals that the binder had scared further in. Terriers would be barking with excitement as a rabbit or rat might suddenly make a break for it and give chase. With a clatter of wings a pheasant or partridge might also fly out. Next job was to stand sheaves into stooks, little stacks, which meant the crop could dry more quickly and gave some protection from showers. There was a real technique to making stooks. 'Always keep the knots on the inside,' said my father. When we were little, my sister Margaret and I could pretend stooks were tiny houses and hide inside. Mother would bring down a picnic of sandwiches and hot tea as the day wore on. Usually you could harvest the sheaves fairly soon if it hadn't rained a lot and take them back on the trailers to the farm where, in the rickyard, a stack would be made.

'A TIME FOR GOSSIPING AND TEA DRINKING'

Making a stack is a real art. For a start it has to stand up and not fall over. My dad and the farm workers we had were good at this but my uncle was not, and if we visited his farm on a Sunday it was interesting to see the variety of wooden props around his sagging stacks. The stacks had to be thatched, just like a house, not to the same standard of course but when it was done the creation was a lovely thing. The thatch was held down by sharp sticks called thatch pegs which made good swords for mock fights when playing soldiers. Thin ones could be used as arrows; we children made our own quite effective bows with willow sticks and string; a good bow would shoot an arrow right over the barn.

In late winter the corn, in the stack, would have dried out naturally, no drying machinery required and then it was time to do the thrashing. The thrasher machine was my uncle's proudest possession. Before the onset of the first safety rules all its wheels, belts and pulleys were exposed, all seemed to be linked and they whirled round as the drum made a great thrumming noise, heard from a long way off. It was driven by a long belt attached to the tractor pulley; ten years before my time the tractor would have been a stationary steam engine. The main thrumming noise came from the thrasher cylinder on top of the drum into which the sheaves from the stack were fed.

The tractor and drum would be fixed into position by metal stakes. All the farm workers and some temporary ones, and kids like me,

would be drafted in to work. At one end of the drum the corn would spill from chutes into hessian sacks and when full, these had to be weighed and tied up with a big needle and string. At the other end of the drum the now seedless straw would be fed into another machine. The chaff was blasted away by a

blower through metal tubes to a place where a chaff pile grew and grew; a great place for playing in later.

Threshing was a bit of a social occasion; time for gossiping and tea drinking. We never had any injuries at Hall Farm but there was an accident in a village some miles away where the person feeding the thresher and standing on top of the drum managed to get his feet chopped off as he slipped into the hole!

After a few days all the threshing would be done and the drum would be put away till next year. Soon the combine harvester appeared and the drum thrummed for the last time in about 1961.

Harvest time, Hall Farm, Osbaston

THE WAR YEARS

IT IS NOW MORE THAN SIXTY YEARS SINCE THE END OF THE SECOND WORLD WAR. ALTHOUGH IT LASTED FOR ONLY SIX YEARS, THESE EXTRACTS REVEAL THAT ITS IMPACT ON LIVES OF INDIVIDUALS IN RURAL ENGLAND WAS IMMENSE. PEOPLE WORKED HARD, USUALLY WITH GOOD HUMOUR, OFTEN IN UNFAMILIAR CIRCUMSTANCES. WOMEN WERE CALLED IN TO DO JOBS, PREVIOUSLY THE WORK OF MEN. THE WAR WAS A TURNING POINT IN THE NATION'S HISTORY AND FOR MANY PEOPLE THE CHANGES WHICH THEY EXPERIENCED WERE BOTH FAR-REACHING AND PERMANENT

Contributors to this section were Jim Lampard, Laura Croman, Blanche Symonds, David Salmon, Patrick Green, Susan Andrews, Gordon and Jill Earp, Martin Shepherd, Dennis Bream and George Armson.

Jim Lampard (butcher) – We were short of meat during the war years and it didn't stop being rationed until 1954. Seth Turner, known as Dick, was a good shop man; he used to keep the customers happy. They would say, 'What have you got to sell us today, Dick?' He would reply, 'I've got elephant and bullyphant'. It was actually corned beef! Apart from a bit of sausage, he had nothing else, but he

managed to keep the customers coming in. My father helped to allocate the meat in Leicester. He had to go in his van on Tuesdays and Thursdays. All the meat was set out in this big arena and he dished it out to the different butchers. When he had done that he had to come home and do his own round in the afternoon. When my father was asked if all the butchers got the same amount of meat he replied, 'No, it all depends on how many ration books are registered with the butcher'.

I think we were about the third or fourth biggest butcher. The biggest butcher was Freeman of Ratby.

Food Office Staff, Southfield Way

'YOU HEARD THOSE DREADFUL MACHINES COMING OVER – THUD, THUD, THUD!'

In the war years we only slaughtered pigs. We killed about ten pigs a week in the winter. Customers fed their own pigs and we would slaughter them on Saturdays or Sundays. One person could only have two pigs. Harry Weston, who used to own the coalyard, would come carrying a bucket with the pig following him. They used to bring pigs from Dadlington and Stoke Golding. The biggest pig we ever killed was from Headley's at Congerstone. When it got to us it had gone through the bottom of the trailer!

When we were killing on Saturdays it all had to be done in a copper tub. The main stoker was Frederick Wain who used to get the fire going and boil the water; three of hot to one of cold that was the mixture to get the hair off.

Laura Croman – When Coventry got bombed it was a bright, moonlit night. It was the harvest moon and they said you could read a paper by it in the fields at Carlton. They bombed and bombed all night. You heard those dreadful machines coming over – thud, thud, thud! They made an entirely different sound to our engines and they bombed Coventry until not much of the old city was left. In the morning, most of the city was closed off so they could get things straight and people and companies had to move out. One company, called Churchill's which made aeroplane components, came to Bosworth. It went into the empty fire station which stood between the Wembley houses and the Council Offices. I worked there and we made valves for aeroplanes. During the worst of the war we only had one afternoon off a week; we had to keep the men in the air.

Blanche Symonds writes: When World War II started we used the house cellar as a shelter. Gas masks were carried in a box at all times and weekly fire drills were held. There was no electricity in the house so light in the cellar was from candles. News of the war was received on a radio run by an accumulator, charged at Kelly's Garage. Rationing continued until the 1950s and we looked forward to using our sweet coupons. The already full house accommodated evacuees from London. Mrs Welsh, Walter Baynes' grandmother, and her daughter, Winnie, stayed for four years in the front rooms of our house.

Above:
The Wembley houses, so called because they were bought from The Exhibition, Wembley 1924, possibly by Timber Fireproofing Co Ltd.

'ITALIAN PRISONERS OF WAR WERE ALLOWED TO COME AND HELP US WITHOUT ANY GUARDS'

David Salmon – The bombing on the night of the Coventry raid was so intense that sleepers at the bottom of the pond at Sedgemere were loosened by the vibration and came to the surface; they almost covered the pond. My father used a dozen of them to build a summerhouse. One of the aircraft lightened its load by dropping a couple of bombs; one at Valley Farm, Tinsel Lane, Wellsborough, and the other in front of Common Farm. The crater in front of Common Farm is still there.

There was a petrol depot on Station Road, and the railway cutting that they provided to transport the petrol, is still there. There were two Akak guns defending it; one was situated at Carlton.

Patrick Green – I had a canoe which I used to paddle along the Ashby canal which ran through Upper Coton Farm. There was a lot of work to do, and Italian prisoners of war were allowed to come and help us in quite a liberal way, without any guards. I certainly remember German prisoners working on other farms being guarded by a soldier with an old .303 rifle. There was a prisoner of war camp in Shady Lane in Leicester, which I remember passing. In fact, I came across one of the former prisoners from there after the war, when I went to Germany to look at some knitting machinery because I had a knitwear factory in Leicester. The boss of the firm I visited had been a prisoner in the camp at Shady Lane and remembered being ordered to 'Dig for Victory' in Victoria Park, Leicester.

Gordon and Jill Earp – We had two Italian prisoners of war working for us on the farm at Thurlaston. They lived in one of the farm cottages. We furnished the cottage and they looked after themselves. I remember they used to like Woodbine cigarettes which Dad bought for them. They didn't have much money but we provided them with food and cigarettes in exchange for their labour. I don't remember them having guards. They were just like any other farm labourers except they didn't have very good English though gradually it improved and they were able to communicate quite well really. They were good workers and good men. They came from the prisoner of war camp at Sutton Cheney. If you wanted extra labour, you could ask for two men for three or four days and they would come every day on their bikes.

Finley (Jim) Salmon at Sedgemere, Station Road

'I THINK SOME OF THE EVACUEES FOUND IT DIFFICULT TO FIT IN WITH COUNTRY LIFE BECAUSE THEY WERE CITY CHILDREN'

Then, of course, there were the land-girls. They were based in Bosworth on Station Road on the left hand side, just before you get to the wooden bungalows.

Dennis Bream writes: During the war, a Defiant which had been shot up crash-landed in the triangular field to the west of Botany Spinney along the Wellsborough Road. Also during the war a Flying Fortress crashed into the willow trees along the brook across the road from Nailstone

THE girls of the Women's Land Army based at the Market Bosworth hostel, in 1947-48.

depot. All the crew were killed and there was debris everywhere. An instruction was also given to farmers to leave farm trailers and equipment out in the bigger fields to stop enemy planes landing. I certainly remember the long field to the left of the Twycross Road at Bilstone with a hay loader, a horse rake and wooden hen pens scattered over it. One day, in about 1943, a barrage balloon which had broken loose, came drifting over Carlton. We heard a Spitfire start up at Desford, which then flew over and shot it down. The balloon burst into flames and came down in the fields near Barton in the Beans.

Gordon and Jill Earp – We weren't short of food. We always had eggs which we could trade for other goods. Dad took the milk from Thurlaston into Leicester every morning. He got an extra halfpenny or penny a gallon for delivering the milk by 7 AM. On his way, he always collected a newspaper. Mum used to send some eggs for them and they used to let us have a tin of golden syrup in exchange which we used on our porridge in the morning.

We had evacuees at Thurlaston who came from London. Thurlaston School wasn't overcrowded; we went to school all day but some schools had morning sessions and an afternoon session for another set of pupils. I think some of the evacuees found it difficult to fit in with country life because they were city children.

I don't think farmers ever went hungry and if they did it was their own fault. We killed pigs, you see, so we always had a lot of fat bacon. We cured our own bacon and hams; they would keep for twelve months. We either took the pigs to the butcher for slaughter or the butcher would come to the farm.

'THE PEOPLE OF BOSWORTH LOOKED AFTER US. THEY COLLECTED MONEY AND THE PUB LOOKED AFTER US'

We used everything of the pig, bar its squeak! The sides of bacon were called flitches and we would hang them on the walls to dry out before we could use them. They were put on thrawls in the old dairies to be cured with salt and saltpetre. They had to lie in brine for quite a while. There was a plughole for draining off the water. My father used to shoot a lot of rabbits and game but I have never shot anything even though I have lived on a farm all my life. Dad would shoot rabbits on our arable land and take them home. People would hear the guns going off and they would queue up for the rabbits.

'MARKET BOSWORTH LADS GAVE A GOOD ACCOUNT OF THEMSELVES FOR THE SIZE OF THE TOWN'

George Armson writes: Our meeting places were mostly on the bank corner or under the lamp on the corner of Main Street and Park Street. On one Sunday the news wasn't good; war had been declared. Many local lads and girls joined up. Sadly, when we came home on leave there would be others who had left to sign up and some who did not return. I, myself, was lucky. I joined the Navy and was on a water gunboat and on a landing-craft as well. One night we were going ashore and I was on Watch when I recognised some local lads. 'What the hell are you doing here?' I said. It was Cyril Cheshire. He and Clarence Bailiss were in the same flotilla as me and there was a lad from Barwell as well. We had the Leicester Regiment on board our boat.

The people of Bosworth looked after us. They collected money and the pub looked after us too. Sid Folwell of the Dixie Arms used to take anybody who was on leave to Leicester, for a day out. One day there were four of us and Sid wanted a photo of us together. Whilst waiting for the photo to be taken an army officer came in, looked at us and said to Sid, 'Are these your four sons, sir?' Sid said, 'Yes'. The officer said, 'Bloody good show, sir. I've only got two.' After that the photo was always known as Sid's Four Sons. It used to be in the bar at the Dixie.

When the war ended and the lads were coming home, it began to hit us that some would not be returning. Market Bosworth lads gave a good account of themselves for the size of the town, as their names show on the War Memorial.

Sid Folwell, centre front with George Armson to his left

'MY MATERNAL GRANDMOTHER WAS SOMETHING OF A CHARACTER, A REAL MOVER AND SHAKER'

Martin Shepherd – I can remember the last two years of the war when we lived at Bosworth, with the soldiers coming to the Black Horse and the Dixie. They were in Gopsall as well and they used to come to Bosworth. I remember the American soldiers up at Bosworth I recall standing outside the Black Horse where the Americans used to give us chewing gum, Wrigley's chewing gum, and I also understood they brought the ladies, nylons.

Towards the end of the war, I remember vividly when barbed wire was rolled across the roads especially down Barton Road. I'm about the only one that does, I think. The wireless vehicles came up to the top of Park Street where the spinney used to be, which is the rose garden now; the three or four wireless vans being along there. I remember standing by them trying to listen to what the soldiers were saying. Policemen walked round Bosworth making sure the shutters were all up so there was no light showing.

One year, on the left-hand side towards the railway station was the army camp. We were taking some cattle down to the station and three or four of them got into the camp. I and some others went in and we were soon held up by the Sergeant Major who was quite upset because we were in there. We explained to him that there were some cattle in there which he didn't know about, until then, so we got them out and got away with it like; we shouldn't have been in there really. They did not have a guard on the gate.

Susan Andrews – My maternal grandmother was something of a character, a real mover and shaker in the very early forties. She was involved in fund raising for the forces; she was involved with the Soldiers, Sailors, Airmen and Families Association (SSAFA). She would go to great lengths to raise money to send to this Association. My grandmother also helped form the Market Bosworth

British Legion Women's Section in 1952. She was on the board of governors of the Dixie Grammar School, the Modern School and a councillor for Bosworth Rural District Council. She even found time to play bowls at Market Bosworth Bowls Club which is still there. In her capacity as school governor, she was also a trustee of the Mistress Hester Hodges, Exhibition Foundation in the parish of Stoke Golding and the Spence's Hospital and Pension Charity for Carleton in Craven which helped underprivileged families, all in the Bosworth area.

Collection for SSAFA, King Bill

BOSWORTH HALL

THE BUILDING OF THE PRESENT HALL COMMENCED IN 1670 WHEN IT WAS THE HOME OF THE DIXIE FAMILY. IN 1885 CHARLES TOLLEMACHE SCOTT PURCHASED THE PROPERTY AND LATER, IN 1918, MR RUDOLPH DELIUS BECAME THE OWNER UNTIL 1931 WHEN IT WAS SOLD TO THE LEICESTERSHIRE COUNTY COUNCIL AND DEVELOPED AS A HOSPITAL. TODAY, OF COURSE, IT IS ONE OF THE BRITANNIA CHAIN OF HOTELS

Contributors to this section were Barbara Arm, Maurice Harris, Ray Carter and Brian Wilson

Barbara Arm writes: At Bosworth Hall lived a wealthy woollen merchant, Mr Rudolph Delius, previous to that Mr Charles Tollemache Scott lived there and owned practically the whole of Bosworth. My mother could remember in her young days when, at Christmas, the old ladies of Bosworth were given a red flannel petticoat. There was a tale that the Squire once saw a woman cleaning her front doorstep with a piece of red flannel, so the Christmas present was discontinued. Also a tale was told that, on walking down Main Street, Carlton, he saw some women gossiping at the front doors of cottages which he owned so the front doors were taken off and moved to face the gardens at the back.

Maurice Harris — I remember my father, Cyril, telling me that when he went to apply for a job at Bosworth Hall, Rudolph Delius said to him, 'I'm sorry I can't employ you; you wear glasses. I can't have bell boys wearing glasses as it doesn't create the right image. However, there is a job in the gardens so you can work there if you like'. He had to find work so went to work in the gardens where eventually he became Head Gardener. He stayed there until the Hall was taken over by the County Council.

Cyril was on duty when he spied a rabbit nibbling the lettuce, so he fetched the gun; forgetting it was a 12 bore he let fire, shot the rabbit but shattered a dozen panes of glass in the greenhouse. He had to spend all Sunday, his day off, puttying-in new glass panes.

Water Tower and kitchen garden

'THEY HAD COME ACROSS A LOT OF SKELETONS IN THE TRENCH WHILST DIGGING FOR THE FOUNDATIONS'

Cyril was still working on the Estate when Squire Delius was the owner. One of his duties as gardener was to provide the house each morning with fourteen perfect new carnations. They had to be new, not yesterday's and they had to be put on the breakfast table before 8 AM. On one occasion he had only got thirteen. So panic - what did he do? What could he do but to put a carnation in from the previous day and that was the end of the story as far as he was concerned. About three days later the lady of the house walked round the gardens, which she did quite regularly, and said to him, 'Oh Cyril, why did we only have thirteen carnations on the table and one from the previous day?' He admitted that unfortunately he was at fault, and was duly reprimanded. For many years he could not understand how that happened, so as a little experiment, we put some carnations in a vase and took one out and put it in a vase with some new ones. The following day we found that fresh carnations developed air bubbles all down the stalks but those a day old had no air bubbles.

In 1932 Cyril was made Head Gardener. They concentrated mainly on vegetables, not flowers with all spare produce at that time, sent to Simpkin & James, a delicatessen in Leicester. He remembered the Wilderness covered in aconites, snowdrops, daffodils and bluebells. One of his jobs in his spare time was to help dig out the stew ponds near to the lake which were then used to breed trout.

Anyway, Bosworth Hall was sold and converted into an infirmary. It took a couple of years before they decided what they were going to do. They built the New Block which accommodated the wards, now Swan House, and they built what was the Nurses' Home but is now St Peter's Court apartment

block. Whilst he was working in the gardens one day, the foreman from the firm building the Nurses' Home came to him and said they were in trouble. They had come across a lot of skeletons in the trench whilst digging for the foundations. There were at least a dozen and asked him to go and have a look. So he went to have a look and sure enough there was a line up of skeletons. I think you could see them from the waist down to the knees in the trench. So between them they decided that they would have to get the authorities involved. They contacted the police first and then the Council. They all gathered round and pontificated for a little while but eventually they decided that a coroner would have to be called and the skeletons would have to be exhumed. Cyril was sworn to secrecy because they didn't want the building of the Nurses' Home to be delayed.

Above: Nurses' Home, now St Peter's Court

'HER SPIRIT HAUNTS THE HALL IN THE FORM OF THE GREY LADY'

Ray Carter writes: A pair of old prison doors from the infamous Newgate Prison in London, given to the early Dixies, was mounted at the doorway to one of the cellar rooms. One of the early Dixies was apparently the Newgate Prison Governor. Along with the mantrap and a coffin, also on display, they provided a gruesome thrill at the Chamber of Horrors exhibition at one of the fêtes organised by the Friends of Bosworth Park Infirmary, to raise money for the hospital.

The mantrap had a tragic story documented to it. The story goes that the 4th Baronet, Sir Wolstan Dixie discovered his daughter, Anna, was having a liaison with a local yeoman farmer's boy. As this would

Details taken from the Sale Catalogue for the Sale of Bosworth Park, 1918:

THE KITCHEN GARDEN

of about two acres and contains a range of Lean-to Cold Fruit Glasshouses in five divisions, also heated Forcing Pits, Melon House, Rose House etc. The Garden is enclosed by a lofty red brick wall with fine wrought iron gates leading into the Park. A large number of choice trees bear an abundant yield of fruit.

The North side of the Kitchen Garden is sheltered by the Water Tower, Gardeners' Bothies, Engine House with pump room,

'THE TRAP CAUGHT ANNA DIXIE WHO LAY THERE ALL NIGHT. HER

INJURIES LED, EVENTUALLY, TO GANGRENE AND SHE DIED'

have been below her station in life, her father was angered and had the mantrap, a vicious spring loaded trap with sharp jaws, set to catch the boy in the copse known as the Wilderness where the couple were known to meet. The trap caught Anna Dixie who lay there all night. Her injuries led, eventually, to gangrene and she died. Since then there has been a rumour that her spirit haunts the Hall in the form of the 'Grey Lady'. State Enrolled Nurse, Margaret Girgens, one of the reunion organisers, claimed to have seen the 'Grey Lady' one night and was terrified. Nurse Jean Jones reports two encounters with an apparition, one seen on the Victorian bridge. The trap is now believed to be in the possession of the Vero family.

boiler house, battery store, etc., the whole of which has been built after the style of the house and makes an imposing addition to the kitchen garden.

THE GARDENS AND GROUNDS

are of the same age as the House, and have a charm that only time can give. On the West side of the House is the formal Entrance Court with its fine Wrought Iron Gates and Broad Steps leading to the Terrace; on the South side, below the Terrace, is an unusually Extensive Lawn, bordered on both sides by large Yews of great age.

Background, entrance gates to Bosworth Hall

'THERE IS A FISHPOND CONTAINING GOOD-SIZED TROUT AND ON THE BANK
A BOARDED AND THATCHED BOAT HOUSE'

The Lawn is separated from the Deer Park
by the Moat, which is guarded by a fine stone
Balustrade, having in the centre a beautiful
Wrought Iron Gate, with steps down to the
water.

On the East side is the old sunk Bowling
Green, now used as Two Tennis Courts; they
are surrounded by fine broad Yew Hedges, the
result of many years' careful attention, the
inner banks are clothed in lavender. Beyond
is the Wilderness, a magnificent Avenue of
Limes and Elms, the ground under which is
carpeted in the Spring with snowdrops,
aconites and bluebells.

The North side is occupied by the Stable Yard,
which in turn is surrounded by a fine
Holly Hedge.

THE OLD DEER PARK

part of which is included in this lot,
is heavily timbered with fine trees, a great
many being oaks. There is a Fishpond
containing good sized trout and on the bank
a boarded and thatched Boat House on
brick foundations, and also in the Park a

Cricket Ground, with small Pavilion.

Deer at Bosworth Hall

BOSWORTH SHOW, CATTLE MARKET AND MAYFAIR

THE BOSWORTH SHOW, NOW HELD IN JULY, HAS A LONG AND INTERESTING HISTORY AS DO THE MAYFAIR AND THE CHRISTMAS FATSTOCK SHOW. THE ONLY SURVIVING EVENT IS THE BOSWORTH SHOW.

The contributors to the Bosworth Show section were Gordon Earp, Laura Croman, John Thorp, Robert Jarvis, Robert Taylor, Peter Loseby and Pat Cooling.

Gordon Earp – The Bosworth Show was first held in 1896 and the founder was Charles Tollemache Scott. He offered the Park as a site for the Show; it was such a wonderful setting.

August bank holiday was a national holiday. The Show was originally held on the Wednesday of August bank holiday week and has only ever been a one-day show. The Show has been held every year with the exception of two breaks; one for World War I and one for World War II.

The Show began with cows, beast, sheep, horses and pigs on exhibition. All types of horses were also shown. Shire horses were always a big attraction as was the Fur and Feather tent which had poultry, rabbits and guinea pigs on display. The Horticultural tent was also very popular. It wouldn't be Bosworth Show without the Atherstone Hunt hounds. The children always liked to run in the ring amongst the hounds.

Agricultural stands in those days consisted of Paynes of Hinckley and Holdrons of Ashby, Freddie Woolf from Nuneaton, Parsons and Sherwin's and probably a few more. Paynes had tractors on show and they used to entertain the customers to a cup of tea or a little drop of the hard stuff.

Laura Croman – Bosworth Show was later moved to the Thursday after August bank holiday Monday and that was the day that set the place alight. Hundreds of people came by bus or, in those days, bicycle. Mrs Towers on Main Street used to store the bicycles in her entry; there were dozens and dozens of bikes.

Showground on Brier Hill, with grandstand

'THEY ALWAYS HAD A SHOW DANCE IN ST PETER'S HALL, BUT THERE USED TO BE A FEW FIGHTS'

The showground was on a large flat field near the Hall. In my early days if a motor vehicle came by everybody went out to have a look at it, as transport was mostly by horse-drawn carriages, and there was much competition for what the horses left behind. Some of the exhibits were walked to the Show; men were to be seen leading bulls through the streets with rings in their noses and held by poles. The best thing, in my opinion, was the Shire horses with their pretty little foals by their sides. They had all been washed and combed and polished; they were beautiful.

We mostly went to the Show in the afternoon as it was very expensive in the mornings but cheaper after 4 o'clock. Two of my brothers used to get up early on the next day to go down to help clear up the showground. This was because when the men came out of the beer tent, they often didn't put their money away properly and there was the odd florin or half-a-crown to be found lying in the grass, if you knew where to look.

As well as the exhibition of farm animals there was also a show tent where people exhibited their produce, cakes, chutneys and jams, all that sort of thing, and prizes were given. Mr Graver, the Headmaster of the Secondary Modern School, often won prizes for his pots of jam.

John Thorp – I used to go up and help put the tents up. Owen Brown, from Loughborough, used to erect the tents and I would go and help for a few days prior to the show; I didn't get paid for it. Bosworth Show was on the first Thursday in August and the weather was often temperamental about that time of year. The field used to get wet and at times, things got bogged down. Towards late afternoon, they had the gymkhana events in the main ring and then in the evening they would have fireworks.

'WHEN THE MEN CAME OUT OF THE BEER TENT THEY OFTEN DIDN'T PUT THEIR MONEY AWAY PROPERLY'

There was a large funfair which went on, probably, until 12 o'clock. They always had a dance in St Peter's Hall, a Show Dance, but there used to be a few fights, about that time, because some of the people spent a lot of time in the pubs during the day. Some people went to the pubs and never went to the Show. I remember somebody playing the spoons in the pub which I hadn't heard before. They used to get buses from all over the area bringing people to the Bosworth Show. It was reputed to be one of the largest one day shows in England, at that time, probably getting from 40-50,000 attending. One of the features was the flower tent which Mr Salmon ran or organised.

Shire horses, Bosworth Show

'SHE CAME DOWN AND IT WAS LULU'

Robert Jarvis – There were fruit tents, flower tents and other large displays. People would go to a lot of trouble and set up a complete garden in the tents, like they do at the Chelsea Flower Show now.

Robert Taylor (publican of the Red Lion Hotel) – We got a phone call saying they had a young lady at the Show who needed to change for her act and was there any chance that we could give her somewhere to change. She came down and it was Lulu. Anyway, she went to change upstairs and was chatting to my father-in-law for about an hour. She gave him a signed photo that he still has with, 'Thanks a lot Bob', on the bottom. He's still got that in an old brown envelope somewhere at home.

'THE BANDS WERE ALL TOP MILITARY BANDS, THE COLDSTREAM GUARDS, THE RAF BAND, ALL BIG BANDS'

Peter Loseby –The beginning of August was like a show week because there was the Abbey Park Show at the start of the week, then the Ashby Show, followed by the Bosworth Show. Ours was the best and the biggest one day show, it was in the top three of one-day shows in the Midlands. It wasn't just a village show; it was a big show with literally thousands attending. As many as 30,000 people would be a poor year. When you consider the population of the village, at that time, probably around 1500, the impact on the village was enormous.

They came from Birmingham and the East and West Midlands, mainly by bus. It wasn't that the buses arrived in the morning and stopped all day, as soon as the passengers were off-loaded they returned for a further bus load. A lot of people also came on push-bikes, as cars were not as common as they are now, car parking wasn't a problem.

The bands were all top military bands, the Coldstream Guards, the RAF Band, all big bands. They used to come on to Bosworth after the Abbey Park Show.

For us, it was an opportunity to earn a bit of pin money as kids, as well as for the men and women in their 20s and 30s. Everyone had a role to play. As a kid I remember having a steward's badge so I was able to go up at 10 AM when it opened and wander around free of charge.

Cattle often came from a distance and I remember that the cattle used to be tied up to the fence in front of the Wilderness. There were pens there for the cattle and they were big cattle - prize bulls!

Showground

'LIGHTNING STRUCK ONE OF THE TOWERS OF THE HIGH WIRE ACT'

The standard of the horse jumping events would be comparable to the Royal Show. The jumping was top notch; Olympic international riders like the Broomes, Harvey Smith and Ted Edgar. Also Colonel Llewellyn came and he was famous for winning the only gold medal in the Olympics on Foxhunter. People used to come and park up and sit five deep, on bales of straw, and just not move an inch, watching the horses jumping all day. I think Dorian Williams was the commentator and he had a caravan with masses of loud speakers.

The village came alive and the King Bill had barrels piled up high because they would shift some beer that day. They used to open at 10 AM and close at 5 PM for an hour, to swill out, and then open again at 6 PM till 11 PM.

The marquees were big and one year, when there was a very bad storm that hit at about 4 PM, everyone got inside the tents. The tents had got to be big to take the thousands that were crammed like sardines beneath the roof which was bowing under the weight of the water. We stood cheek by jowl and I was scared to death, hiding beneath my mother's skirt. I was too young to realise that the tons of water could have collapsed the tent and cause death. This happened during a high-wire act when a guy on a bike rode to the middle of a wire, suspended between two thin towers. He used a long pole to give balance and hanging beneath him, a girl did acrobatics on a trapeze.

It was only afterwards that we found out that in amongst one of these loud cracks of thunder, there was lightning that struck one of the towers on the high wire. This lightning charge of electricity travelled into the ground, lifted up a local man, Jack Jones, and threw him to the back of the President's tent. He was lucky to get away with it unharmed. Jack was a well-known Bosworthian who was the leader of the Leicestershire miners.

Galliford's horse-drawn bus, Bosworth Show

'THERE WAS A GUY IN MY DAY, KEN MATTHEWS, WHO CAME FROM SUTTON COLDFIELD AND WAS AN OLYMPIC CHAMPION'

Those folks who had been unable to get into the tents and had been under the cypress trees, or wherever they could get shelter, were drenched. There were no drying facilities and the ground was a bog. Big tractors had to hoick the fair out the next day; they were up to ankle deep in mud.

The firework display used to start at about 8.30 PM with a maroon rocket; no stars or anything, just a great big bang that shook the ground. There weren't just half a dozen people, there was row after row, and you looked back and there was a sea of people. Of course they had to put on an aerial display and the final thing was always the waterfall.

There were athletic and cycling events on the field and a road walk, all of which were very popular. I was heavily involved in the seven mile road walk. There was a guy in my day, Ken Matthews, who came from Sutton Coldfield and was an Olympic champion. Another competitor was Don Thompson, known as Mighty Mouse, and he was a 20 kilometre walker. He won gold in Rome. At the end of the race, my brother or I would, on our bikes holding a blue flag, lead the winner on to the field and the finishing line.

There was one chap, named Mr Tempest, who was bald and brown as a berry. He came from Blackpool every year and was still coming to Bosworth Show when he was eighty. He was a magical guy because I swear that he would have a smile on his face when he set off and he got the same smile on his face when he got back. He was always near the back coming in to finish but he used to wear a white vest and black shorts and got to be known by the crowds. They used to cheer him to the hilt, as he came through the showground to the announcement, 'Here he comes!' He used to get a real big cheer.

3.0 p.m. ROAD WALK, EIGHT MILES HANDICAP

First Home £7-7-0. Second £5-5-0. Third £3-3-0.

Handicap Prizes, £5-5-0, £4-4-0, £2-2-0.

First Novice, 30/-. First Veteran (over 45) 30/-.

ROAD WALKING OFFICIALS

Judges:

T. P. Clarke (*Chief*), E. Kemp, J. W. Billson, W. Bell, W. A. Cooke, C. F. Hewitt, S. C. Packer, C. A. Brockhouse, A. E. Aldridge, A. P. Deighton, A. R. Downing.

Recorders: F. Betts, J. Lowe.

Timekeepers: E. L. Wood, M. Long.

MARKET BOSWORTH 1959

Handicap Allowances compiled by A. H. Johnson. Hon. Handicapper, R.W.A. Midland Area, up to July 18th.

NOTE.—Competitors will complete 2¾ laps at start of walk and ¾ to finish it.

No.	Name and Club	Handicap M.	S.
141	K. J. Matthews, Royal Sutton W.C.	Scratch	
142	F. Winter, Sheffield U.H.	4	20
143	M. Greasley, Sheffield U.H.	4	30
144	A. H. Poole (V.), Worcester H.	4	50
145	D. B. Greasley, Sheffield U.H.	5	00
146	L. Radford, Sheffield U.H.	5	00
147	F. C. Brookes, Lozells H.	5	10
148	R. Ibbotson, Sheffield U.H.	6	00
149	M. Bingley, Sheffield U.H.	6	00
150	A. Rozentals, Royal Sutton W.C.	6	30
151	J. Bonnington, Sheffield U.H.	7	00
152	P. Markham, Leicester W.C.	7	00
153	F. O'Reilly, Lozells H.	7	30
154	J. H. T. Eddershaw, Sheffield U.H.	8	00
155	B. J. Russell, Gosport A.C.	8	20
156	J. A. Dowling, Sheffield U.H.	8	30
157	A. Butler, Leicester W.C.	9	30
158	S. R. Mantor (V.), Enfield A.C.	9	30
159	N. Hopkinson (V.), Sheffield U.H.	9	30
160	C. R. Hooper, Basingstoke A.C.	10	00
161	K. Woodward (N.), Sheffield U.H.	11	30
162	J. M. Smith (N.V.), Stourbridge & Wordsley H.	11	30
163	B. Harby (N.), Melton A.C.	11	30
164	R. I. M. Purkis, R.A.F. Henlow	12	00
165	G. R. Tarall, Leicester W.C.	12	00
166	D. F. Osman (N.), Southampton A.C.	13	00
167	T. G. R. Sharlott, Leicester W.C.	13	30
168	G. Hall, Royal Sutton W.C.	13	30
169	R. A. Woodcock, Leicester W.C.	14	00
170	G. A. Mitchell, Birmingham W.C.	15	00
171	A. Cooper (N.), Leicester W.C.	17	00
172	V. R. Wilson, Worcester H.	17	30
173	A. J. Tompkinson, Leicester W.C.	18	00
174	B. Osborn (V.), Birmingham W.C.	19	00
175	J. Curtis (V.), Sheffield U.H.	19	00
176	J. Tempest (V., born 1880), Lancashire W.C.	35	00

1st............. 2nd............. 3rd............. Time.............

'IF YOU WERE LUCKY YOU WOULD FIND TWO SHILLINGS OR HALF-A-CROWN'

Everyone went to see the flowers in the horticultural tent. There were famous exhibitors like Harry Wheatcroft with his roses. Finley Salmon used to have a rock garden with water features. I can remember trying to figure out how fountains could be in there, I didn't understand about pumps and reservoirs then. Another tent had vegetables on display and the Towers brothers used to win a lot; they were local lads, and you would see their names on a regular basis.

The next day we used to go picking up all the rubbish and we were paid by the sack load. There were no gloves or anything, you just dived in, you didn't bother about bits of glass, you picked it all up but it was the money you found, sixpences and threepenny bits and pennies and if you were lucky you would find two shillings or half-a-crown.

Pat Cooling –Freda Jackson used to arrange an after Show Day Dance in aid of Sunday School funds.

My sister, Ann, took part in the high-wire act at the Show with the Diaboloes. They asked if they could piggyback her across on the wire; she was only about eleven or twelve. I don't know how she dare do it, but she did, and I can remember Dad going into the tent and asking Mum if she was going to come and see her but she wouldn't go and watch. Dad was the Secretary to the Show Committee; they called him Jim, in Bosworth, but his name was actually Finley. Preparations began in May and it was very much hands on, for the family.

Ann used to go up after work and type out all the labels for everything. She would be typing and my mother would be folding the bills; handbills to go out everywhere. Everything had to be typed and when my sister went, I had to do it.

CATTLE MARKET

The Cattle Market has always been central to life in Market Bosworth. Its history goes back to 1861.

Contributors to this section were:
Laura Croman, Gordon Earp, Robert Jarvis, Roger Payne and Martin Shepherd.

Laura Croman – Years ago an annual Horse Fair was held which attracted professional drovers wearing their traditional kerchiefs and wielding their pliable ash stick. Sometimes they were paid tokens which they exchanged at the Black Horse for food and drink. The selling stock for later years was bulls, cows, calves, many sheep and pigs.

Mr Smith and Mr Shepherd at rear of the Black Horse

'THE REV TEDDY BOSTON CARVED THE JOINT COOKED BY MRS DYKE'

The privately owned sale ground was acquired by Orchard and Joyce, then Nixon, Toone & Harrison in the 1930s. Later, the Hackney family came into the partnership. Old Joe Hackney lived to be over 100 years old and made an appearance at the market to celebrate his birthday.

The heyday of the business was in the 1950s and 60s. To alert the customers in the grounds,

a large bell was sounded in the Black Horse Tap Room, before selling commenced. As well as farmers, the sale attracted as many as twenty butchers. Treatment of animals was less humane in those days and suckling pigs, bought to fatten up, were carried for miles across the shoulders, or on a bicycle, squirming and squealing in a sack.

Two brothers, called Smith, from Cumberland, regularly brought short-horned bulls to the Mayfair. If the boys were brave enough, like Harry Trivett, they could earn sixpence per animal to escort them to market from the station.

For some years, Melton and Stilton cheeses were sold by a local man from the back of his car. Wilf Spencer, son of the Black Horse landlord, sold eggs. One day, misjudging the entrance gateposts in his horse and trap, it overturned to the detriment of his goods!

Cattle food, implements, tools and other farmers' requisites could be obtained to order. A weighing machine was once sited in the Square, looked after by Mr Flude, the saddler, and later by Mrs Beck. The Cattle Market became a self-contained unit with easy access for food and drink, via the pub's back door. In the later years the auctioneer's staff

went across to Bakery Cottage where the Rev Teddy Boston carved the joint cooked by Mrs Dyke.

During the war years, the Market became a grading station where farmers had to present their animals for inspection by a Ministry of Food official, although some grading is known to have taken place prior to this.

The highlight of the year was always the Christmas Fatstock Market and Poultry Sale. In 1969 a committee was formed, chaired by Mr Sam Heath, to award trophies for the Best in Class and Best in Show.

Above: Cattle Market
Right: David Fox and Gordon Earp

'SOMETIMES THE CATTLE WOULD JUMP OVER A FENCE INTO SOMEONE'S GARDEN'

Gordon Earp – The Mayfair was held in the Cattle Market for two days. Cows sold on the first day and bulls, and one and two-year old stock beast on the second day. Bulls were brought down from Cumbria on the train by Mr Smith. Butchers usually entertained the regular customers. A funfair was held for two days in the Market Place at the same time.

Laura Croman – The May funfair was held in the Square and came on the first Wednesday and Thursday after May Day. There were roundabouts, coconut stalls, swings and all that sort of thing. I still have a dish that was won by a friend of my father who was a champion darts player. My father talked him into having a go at one of the stalls to win me the best prize, much to the stall holder's disgust.

Robert Jarvis – We had the local Mayfair when the farmers would bring what they call store-cattle to the market. As young lads, there were quite a few Bosworth boys who would go to the market and the dealers there would say, 'Here is two bob, my lad, would you help us run these cattle down to the station?' So all the cattle would be put into one pen and then be driven through the Market Place and down Station Road. On occasion things wouldn't go according to plan and sometimes the cattle would jump over a fence into someone's garden. That involved getting shouted at, to get the cattle out of the garden. Eventually, we would get about 98% down to the station yard where they were put into pens and loaded onto trains to Birmingham, or wherever they were going.

After the cattle market there was the May funfair which was held in the Market Place. This had side shows, dodgems, roundabouts and things like that. This went on for three days, which was quite an episode when you lived in the Market Place because there was no chance of going to bed early, as the fair never closed before eleven or twelve o'clock at night.

May funfair, Market Place

'SOME FARMERS NEVER WENT OUT ALL WEEK BUT WOULD COME UP HERE ON A MONDAY. IT WAS THEIR LIFE'

There was always a Christmas Fatstock Show in Bosworth, to which all the farmers would bring their best cattle, sheep and pigs. It was a great achievement to win that. For a few years Mr Lampard did buy the champion beast which was slaughtered and hung for people to look at. Regulations stopped us hanging carcasses in the shop because they weren't refrigerated. We would go to a farm and buy a complete pen of a hundred or so old hens, take them back to the butchers and pluck and dress them. I think they were about ten shillings then.

Roger Payne – When I started working with David Johnson in 1973, I suggested we had a shed on

Cattle Market, Market Bosworth   164S

the Bosworth Market. From that shed we sold small agricultural requirements. It was just a normal cattle market, the highlight being the annual Fatstock Show held in December and an annual Pumpkin Show, which took place at the back of the Black Horse Inn. Farmers competed to see who could grow the biggest pumpkin. Well, you see a lot of the Market premises belonged to the brewery. Half of the Cattle Market site, I think, belonged to Ind Coope and the other half of the Market belonged to Hackney, the auctioneers. They

used to start with sundries first, odds and ends, then the calves, then the sheep and lambs and finish off with the cattle. The other excitement was the police sale when they sold lost property, about once every six months.

Martin Shepherd – My grandma, Mrs Spencer, kept the Black Horse for thirty odd years. She supplied meals on a Monday for all the farmers and the cattle dealers, as she did

when it was Mayfair day. Grandma scrubbed the floors everyday on her hands and knees, the passage went through from the main door, everyday she did them. She worked really hard and brought up seven children. It was hard work. You see, years ago we all came up to Bosworth; it was a day out for the farmers. Some farmers never went out all week but would come up here on a Monday. It was their life. You see, when the Cattle Market finished, the domino players kept going; there was always about seven or eight of them coming every Monday. I used to go occasionally, then slowly one or two died off and then, when the Black Horse went to all food, they kicked us out. We tried it down the King William but that didn't work very well.

Above: Cattle Market
Right: Black Horse, early 20th century

'I HAVE NOT HAD THE BEST OF DAYS TODAY. I THINK EVERYBODY IS GOING
TO FRIESIANS, I THINK I SHALL STOP COMING'

On the Monday market you would get sixty or seventy fat cattle, in those days, and a few hundred
sheep, as well as pigs, calves and poultry. They were kept in the cattle pens behind the Black Horse.
The Market finished, I think, in 1994. The Mayfair was a two-day market, originally, but then it went
to a one- day sale and, eventually, to alternative Thursdays. I bought the last two animals that were
sold in Bosworth Market.

There was an annual sheep sale in September; we
used to get a few hundred sheep from all over the
district. The Christmas Fatstock day was held mostly
in the second week of December. That was a big day
at Bosworth and it was well supported. Everybody
showed their top cattle and tried to win the champion
beast and champion sheep and pigs et cetera. They
sold poultry dressed and alive. The Young Farmers
had their Young Farmers' competition as well at
Christmas and that was for a Young Farmers' twelve
month old Christmas calf. I won it three times; got a
cup, and one year our family nearly got one, two and three but somebody beat us to third place so my
sister ended up with fourth, else we could have cleared the board. Quite pleased about that really.

The first day of the Fair, the two-day Fair, used to be dairy cattle and bulls and there was a gentleman,
named Mr Will Smith that brought bulls all the way from Pleasington, near Blackburn. I think when
he first started, they came on the train and he had a brother who brought bulls down as well. For quite
a few years they brought Hereford and Shorthorn bulls and did quite well selling them. Mr Smith used
to stop with my grandma at the Black Horse. Then one year, when everybody was turning to British
Friesians, he told her, 'I have not had the best of days today. I think everybody is going to Friesians so
I think I shall stop coming', and he did. He was a lovely chap, Mr Will Smith. You are talking about
twenty to twenty five bulls easy and we used to put them in the sheds that were up at the Black Horse.
Some used to go in there and the surplus ones would be under the shed on the market. His brother
came with him. I don't think they were connected, as far as selling was concerned. They used to bring
some nice bulls and had quite a successful time at Bosworth for a few years. Interesting for us little
ones waiting for the bulls to come, we really enjoyed it. The second day of the Mayfair was mostly,
what we called store-cattle, for grazing on and they would come from quite a wide area to buy those.
You see, in them days there were a lot of outlying cattle, that means cattle that never come in, and
there were some buyers who came just to buy outlying cattle and Bosworth was a good market for
that. There could be quite a few hundred on the second day; it was the biggest day. They came from
Loughborough, Rugby and as I say, the one from the train. I think he came from Worcester way to
buy a lot. Buyers came from quite a long way to Bosworth Fair, years ago.

Martin Shepherd with the last two animals sold in Bosworth Market

BOSWORTH PARK INFIRMARY

AFTER PURCHASE OF BOSWORTH HALL IN THE 1930S, BY LEICESTERSHIRE COUNTY COUNCIL, WORK STARTED ON CHANGING THE HALL INTO THE BOSWORTH PARK INFIRMARY. THE PLANS INCLUDED A NEW TWO-STOREY BUILDING WHICH ACCOMMODATED WARDS AND A TWO-STOREY NURSES HOME. THE HOSPITAL WAS OPENED IN 1936 BY SIR ARTHUR HAZELRIGG, HAVING 177 BEDS FOR THE CHRONICALLY SICK. THE HALL IS THE 17TH CENTURY MANSION BUILT BY THE DIXIE FAMILY WITH 19TH CENTURY ADDITIONS, IN QUEEN ANNE STYLE, BY THE TOLLEMACHE SCOTT FAMILY

BPI Staff who contributed to this history were nurses Reg and Nancy Sperry, Marjorie Vero, Arthur Rowlinson and Ray Carter.

Ray Carter writes: Several hundred babies were delivered each year from the nineteen maternity beds until the Hospital's closure in 1987. The special needs children were dealt with by a physiotherapist and a speech therapist from Leicester, under the Sheffield Health Authority. The Hospital also catered for geriatrics, the chronic sick, convalescent patients and military personnel, some REME *(Royal Electrical and Mechanical Engineers)* based at Gopsall Hall. The Hospital also carried out minor operations on children, with specialists, such as a surgeon and an anaesthetist, travelling from Leicester for ear, nose and throat operations. The anaesthetic used, in the early days, was ether poured over a cotton pad.

Park Infirmary, Market Bosworth.

Matron was in charge of all the nursing staff with strict rules for patient access and caring. Three Matrons covered the life period of the BPI: Miss Mabel M Stringer, 1936-49; Miss Mabel Wilson, 1949-59 and Miss Alice Mole 1959-87. Matron Mole ensured lifts were installed to save stretchering patients down the stairs.

Top left: Bosworth Park Infirmary
Right: Child patients

'FATHERS OF THE NEW BORN BABIES COULD NOT KISS THEIR CHILD, OR THE MOTHER'

Visiting was allowed twice weekly and at weekends but not with children. No one was allowed to sit on beds. Fathers of the new born babies could not kiss their child, or the mother, and relatives were restricted even more so; a practice introduced to protect the patients and babies from infection. These precautions had to be put in place because, at that time, there was a large nationwide increase in gastric infections. Nursing staff had to change from their uniforms before leaving the hospital grounds.

Dr Gordon D Kelly, who resided at nearby Beech House in Church Street, was the Hospital Medical Officer. Reports from staff attest to his attitude and high work ethics. I was the Secretary from 1937 to 1984, apart from serving in the Navy in World War II. My assistant, Bill Rose, came straight from college in 1938 and stayed until 1968, when he was appointed Secretary at Hinckley Hospital.

A Friends of Bosworth was formed in 1956 to cover both Bosworth Park Infirmary and Westhaven, a group made up of many local people and others to support the work of the hospitals, by visits, help and comforts, et cetera. Gifts provided for Bosworth Park Infirmary included a cordless radio

headphone system and most of the ward televisions. There were six wards one of which was St Agnes' Ward, affectionately known as Aggy's. This ward was upstairs in the Mansion and was for geriatric women. It may have been called that after a saint. Coincidently, it was Lady Agnes Tollemache Scott who enabled her husband to purchase and improve Bosworth Hall and Estate in the 19th century and she was revered by her employees and locals for her kind work.

Nurses were housed in the stylish Nurses' Home, now St Peter's Court, within the grounds of the Hall or in the Dower House, a short distance away, and some lived locally. Matron had a suite on the ground floor of the Nurses' Home.

Top right: Bosworth Park Infirmary
Above: Nurses' Home

'THERE'S THIS YOUNG BOY WITH HIS ARM HANGING DOWN. HE HAD BEEN SHOT'

A staff Social Club was formed with dances and fancy dress parties being organised in the BPI Recreation Room which was built over the stores, with a specially constructed maple-wood dance floor. Outings were made to the Royal Horticultural Show at the Chelsea Barracks, to Coventry for

the pantomimes, Wickstead Park and other venues for staff and some patients, usually in Clarence Coaches of Barton. A variety of sports activities were available including tennis on a hard court, two grass courts, a putting green on the south lawn, with walking and cycling groups.

Nancy Sperry – I started training as a State Enrolled Nurse at Market Bosworth Park Infirmary in 1945. Training should have taken two years but was interrupted because they were changing the wards to accommodate injured war soldiers. After one month's probation I went for training to the County Infirmary at Louth.

Most nursing staff lived in the Nurses' Home or in the Mansion; night staff on the top floor of the Nurses' Home and in the Dower House. Bosworth Park Infirmary was considered one of the best training schools for the State Enrolled Nurses, at that time, and I think, actually, it was good nursing.

Marjorie Vero – I was an SEN at the BPI from 1959 to 1987 and had to do my training at the BPI and twelve week stints at Hinckley. I left Westhaven for the BPI taking a substantial drop in salary. I worked on the wards at BPI. One particular morning, I was on with my friend Margaret and all at once she shouted, 'March!' that's how you called one another. I thought, oh, somebody has had an accident in the kitchens, because she was up by the kitchens there and, of course, I thought someone had a bad cut or something. I went up and there's this young boy with his arm hanging down. He had been shot.

Top: Social Club badge
Right: Staff at Bosworth Park Infirmary

'WE HAD TO LET THE BLOOD FLOW AGAIN AND THAT WAS DREADFUL FOR THE POOR LAD'

He had been shot at Gopsall Park and, of course, if one of the other people had been on duty they would have said, no we don't take casualties. Margaret Dix opened the door and she said, 'Well we are not supposed to take casualties, however', she said, 'come on in we will have a look at you anyway'. I went and I thought, Oh my God! I said, run for the blankets, because we hadn't got a bed or anything. We got the lad down on the floor and I asked Rose Stokes to phone for Dr Brittain. He wasn't the hospital doctor any more, he used to be, but he wasn't at that particular time. He said to Rose that he didn't come up there. Rose said, this is an outpatient, so up he came. By that time we had cut his entire jacket away and released the tourniquet. We didn't know how long it had been on so had no choice, we had to let the blood flow again and that was dreadful for the poor lad. The ambulances were on strike.

Mr McKinley commended both of us for what we did because we helped to save the lad's arm. The poor lad wasn't in a fit state and couldn't have gone on to the Royal in his condition. The doctor administered morphine and this helped him on his journey.

We had to do all our lectures in our own time. When you were on nights, sitting up till half past twelve, you used to go cross-eyed looking at the tutors, Mr Lawler and Mr Hilton. We were so tired. I used to get up at about 4 PM to get my dinner; the nurses that lived in didn't get up till half past six. We worked forty eight hours a week and, one week had one and a half days off, and the next week, two days off. When you were on nights, you had a three-night and a two-night stint. I didn't like night duty and at that particular time, if you worked on the convalescent ward, it was your duty to go and call the nurses in the morning, at half past six. There were no street lights and we had to go down to the Dower House and unlock the door, ready for when the night nurses came off duty. I didn't like that duty as we had to go on our own through the churchyard to the Dower House.

St Nicholas Ward

'OH MATRON IT'S A NEW BORN BABE AND IT'S GOT A WONDERFUL NAME, VICTORIA'

When I was in charge of St David's, a male ward, a patient had a visitor carrying a baby which was against the regulations. Because they were from the fairground and the fair was moving on, I bent the rules and allowed the visit but told them to be brief. No sooner had the visitor entered the ward when up the stairs comes Matron. I was on duty with Freda Rowlinson at the time, the other enrolled nurse. I was in trouble and hoped that if I took Matron to the other end, Freda would have grasped the situation and told the visitors that Matron was on the ward and they must leave.

'NO ONE DARED TO DRINK TOO MUCH AS MATRON AND MR CARTER WERE OFTEN PRESENT'

No such luck, when Matron and I finally arrived, there's the visitor still sitting with the baby and I said, Oh Matron it's a new born babe and it's got a wonderful name, Victoria. Well, Matron went into raptures about this baby and nothing was ever said about children on the ward, I got away with it.

Reg Sperry was in a medical unit in World War ll and in 1945 joined the BPI, and did his nursing training there and retired from the BPI after thirty seven years. Reg and Nancy Sperry between them spent a total of around seventy years at the BPI.

Reg Sperry – The social life at the BPI centred mainly around the Recreation Room; a large room situated above the boiler house and food store, big enough for dances, pantomimes and parties. This area had a stage at one end and a small bar in the opposite corner. The beautiful polished floor made it ideal for dances. The bar facilities were usually handed over to the Red Lion landlord for the night. No one dared to drink too much as Matron and Mr Carter were often present. Music for dancing was provided by Ivor Pope and his five piece band.

One of my memories is of sponsored walks we organised, during summer evenings. We would proceed down Shenton Lane, through Sutton Cheney and down the gated road, back to Bosworth which was quite a walk. Both this and the Autumn Fayre held in the front hall and supported well by staff and visitors were efforts to raise money, both for the patients and staff, at Christmas. It was important that each patient had at least one present at Christmas and the money raised helped towards this.

The Social Club would arrange coach outings for the staff and friends throughout the year to places such as Blackpool Illuminations, Ladies Day at Ascot and other places of interest. Clarence Coaches of Barton in the Beans always provided an excellent service for such occasions.

Arthur Rowlinson writes: I was born 27th April 1933, and lived at Nailstone when I was young, and was at BPI from 1948 till 1988, as maintenance engineer.

'ALL THE TREES IN THE GROUNDS USED TO COME ALIVE, ABOUT THAT TIME, WITH PEOPLE SAYING THEIR GOOD NIGHTS'

The good set of stokers at BPI kept the brass and copper pipe work polished with Brasso and spirit of salts, if really dirty. The Solid Fuel Advisory Board used to come to assess us occasionally and we were awarded stars for efficiency. Four stokers, with two days off a week, stoked the furnace with coal-doubles, at a couple of shovels every few minutes, into hoppers. Eighteen tons of coal were used a week, mainly coming from Desford as the coal was considered to be a better quality.

Mr Loseby, whilst working for Frears of Leicester, helped to fit the boilers and when the job was completed, he stayed on to make sure everything went smoothly and then asked to stay permanently. Mr Loseby and myself mainly did the maintenance work on the boilers which were taken down once a year and inspected.

We had a stoker who only came for about a week because the mortuary was close to the boiler house and he couldn't cope with it.

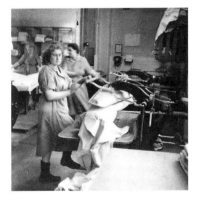

Mr Loseby, a lovely chap to work for, treated me like a son. He only worked days, starting at 9 AM until he went home. I never heard him raise his voice to anyone. Mr Loseby used to take part in the pantomimes that were held there, before my time.

A lot of local lads courted the nurses up there. Locking-up time at the Nurses' Home was about 10 PM, all the trees in the grounds used to come alive about that time, with people saying their good nights.

There was a 60,000 gallon water tank under the orchard. It was needed to keep the laundry going when the mains water was off. We used to pump it up into the tanks, for the laundry, with an electric pump. The tank was fed by natural drainage and a spring. We built an island in the moat with a fountain on it. I used an old tin bath with some outrigger tanks, to get across to it. At the end, near where the tennis courts are, there was a wooden plug with an iron staff coming out of it, with a ring on top. We had to plug the moat once when it leaked, with clay that was brought in.

Top: Mr Loseby in the Boiler House
Above right: Laundry Room

COMMUNITY

MEMORIES OF MARKET BOSWORTH WOULD NOT BE COMPLETE WITHOUT MENTIONING THE COMMUNITY SPIRIT THAT HAS ALWAYS BEEN CENTRAL TO LIFE IN THE TOWN. AS COMMUNITY TUTOR, FOR MANY YEARS, DAVID FITT IS ONE OF THE PEOPLE WHO WAS INSTRUMENTAL IN INITIATING MANY COMMUNITY PROJECTS

The contributor to this section was David Fitt.

David Fitt became Community Tutor in 1976, having first taught geography and PE in Coalville for 2½ years and then PE at South Charnwood in Markfield, after which he became vice-principal at Market Bosworth Community College after it received Community College status. At that time there were not many community classes but he does remember carrying sewing machines to Sheepy Magna

and organizing keep fit at Twycross, painting, dressmaking and tailoring classes at Cadeby. Amongst the groups that met at Bosworth were the Gardening Club and the Bosworth Society, both of which still flourish. Other groups used the Community College: British Legion, Young Farmers' and many other weekly evening classes. As Community Tutor he was involved with the original Aspect Magazine and would deliver to all the surrounding villages. It finally folded in 1991, but David was instrumental in re-launching the magazine, as New Aspect in 1992, due to popular demand.

David Fitt, in collaboration with Ted Jenkins, Headmaster of the school, formed a small committee and organised the first Market Bosworth Carnival week in the late 1970s. This became an annual event for a number of years. He has marvellous memories of this annual event and as the Carnival flourished with success, it became possible to pay for major attractions, as well as marching bands on Carnival days. One year the Essex Dog Display Team was the highlight of the day's festivities. Months before the Carnival, a skittle knock-out competition was held in the King Bill skittle-alley, and with eight in a team and fifty teams, it took two months to complete. It was organized by Gwen Grinsberg, primary school 'Lollipop Lady', for many years.

The WI float

'THEY OPENED THE BOOT, PICKED ME UP, THREW ME IN, JUMPED BACK IN, AND THE CAR ROARED OFF'

David Fitt – I remember the Carnival pram race, when my daughter was about two and there would be five hundred to six hundred people up in the Square. It was absolutely brilliant! They used to stop the traffic and would have the two pram races. This one particular year, after the pram races, when everybody was still there, a white car, which had been parked down Sutton Lane, roared into the Square, lights on, blowing the hooter, screeching to a halt, doors opened and out stepped these people dressed as Arabs firing imitation guns. They ran towards me with a sack and just before they put the sack over my head, I looked round. Nobody had moved, everyone stood there with mouths open. They opened the boot, picked me up, threw me in, jumped back in, and the car roared off. My daughter sobbed, but I soon returned on a push float, dressed as the Carnival Queen. The perpetrators were Michael Dilks, Eddie Keats and a third person. They told me on the day that they were going to do it. I remember going round the Red Lion corner on two wheels shouting, it's not for real!

On Sunday afternoons six-a-side cricket matches were held on the school field after the Carnival, and one year the ball was hit really high by Pete Heath and it dropped straight through the canteen roof.

I remember going to a course, 'Mammals', set up in co-ordination with Leicester University, at Twycross Zoo where the tutor was Jack Otter. Around this time the Bosworth Project was initiated when about £13,000 was raised for the building of a new Sports Hall, a project in which I was heavily involved. Money was raised with coffee mornings, cake stalls, snooker competitions, as well as projects at the school which the children were involved

in, and a fortnightly disco with a hundred or more children at each event. Another major project was the building of the Youth Wing when I ran lunch time meetings for the Year 9 children and where Faye Harvey was the Youth Tutor for nine years. It was the youth involvement that saved my job when Leicestershire County Council withdrew funding for all adult tutors. I made front page of the Coalville Times when people were trying to save his job. The headline was, 'Keep Fitt in Bosworth', and they did. Other plays on names in Bosworth were: Mr Mapp, geography teacher, Miss Cash dealt with finance, Colemans who were coalmen and John Messenger who was the postman!

A winter care programme was set up by me, whereby older members of the population would be looked in on, by a volunteer in their street. If anything was needed I would be contacted and this ran for a number of years with someone nominated in every street. This was initiated during the power cuts and I was asked to provide blankets for Bosworth Court Nursing Home!
I used to go down to the sports ground to meet John Smith and help carry out repairs to the changing facilities. No-one played there, other than the ladies hockey team. He called a meeting in the Dixie Arms to discuss the formation of a football club and a committee of six decided to join the Nuneaton Bible League and later, as a result of the great response, a reserve side joined the League. A regular cricket team also formed after the folding of the Barton in the Beans Club. I was also involved with the Market Bosworth Rugby Club in the formation of the mini-section, where I served as a coach for about eight years.

'HOW ON EARTH IT NEVER WENT THROUGH ONE OF THOSE HOUSES I DO
NOT KNOW TO THIS DAY'

Along with other local men I assisted in the erection of the Christmas tree. I got involved from the
very early days when the Christmas tree often used to come from Mid-Wales. It was brought by

Mr Rickard and Mr Rickard was
nearly always late.

Harry Whitehead and I used to
put the Christmas tree up, and
this was in the time when the
market stalls all used to be left in
the Market Place. We used to get
some of the metal bars and lay
them out, propped the Christmas
tree on them, put the lights on,
and then wait until about 1.30 PM
on the Sunday, when the Sunday
football team came out of the
King Bill, by which time the
ropes were on and then we all
pulled the tree up and slotted it in the hole. How on earth it never went through one of those houses I
do not know to this day.

As the College grew, there was a programme of over fifty classes a week. When asked to do a survey
of how many people went through in a week, County Hall picked the week and we had to do a head
count which did not include any of the children in the High School. It was found that there were
seventeen hundred people going through that place, in a week.

Things have changed a lot now; it's not even a Community College. With the re-organisation by
Leicestershire County Council, obviously the funding has gone from adult education and there are
fewer classes. Classes have been forced out, or moved out, and there is a lack of car parking spaces
during the day. Some classes have moved out to the Rugby Club and places like that. Fortunately the
Sports Hall is still well used which is good, in view of the fact that a Sports Council Grant of £10,000
was given, on the condition that it was open to the public. Having spent thirty years at the College, I
was sad to see the decline in the use of the Community College. However, I enjoyed it at the time, as
did many other people.

The burying of the Millennium Time Capsule in the Parish Field, David Fitt, left foreground

BOSWORTH BITES AND CHARACTERS

A NUMBER OF INTERESTING FACTS AND STORIES CAME TO LIGHT THAT DID NOT FIT NEATLY INTO ANY OF THE CHAPTER HEADINGS. IT WAS FELT THAT THEY WERE TOO VALUABLE TO BE OMITTED SO HAVE FOUND THEMSELVES IN THIS CHAPTER OF MISCELLANEOUS ITEMS.

Contributors to this section were Barbara Arm, Laura Croman, Robert Jarvis, Winifred Smith, Peter and Sheila Loseby, Brian Oakley, Olive Hicklin, Angela Hutton, Paul Oakley and Martin Shepherd.

Barbara Arm writes: At one time a herd of deer roamed the park. It was a beautiful sight to see them feeding in the early morning when we went to school.

At the gate, near to the Primary School, children would stand and open it for the horses and carts coming through. The children were thrown pennies or half-pennies to open the gate. However, on one occasion, a small boy, by the name of Fred Hextall, who was about eight years old, was killed by one of the vehicles. After this incident the children were no longer allowed to continue the practice. They would spend the pennies at the small shop opposite the school to buy sweets. This shop was run by an old lady who also collected the newspapers from the milk train at the station in a small hand truck and she would then deliver them on the way back to her home.

In spring or summer the 'Atora Suet' wagon came round; this was similar to a gypsy caravan and was pulled by two oxen. Sometimes a man would come with a barrel organ. I cannot remember any of his tunes but there was always a monkey attached to the organ and we would stand and gaze at this wonderful sight. A large handle was turned to produce the music.

There was also a scissor-grinder who would come round occasionally. The scissors were ground on a stone wheel that worked on a foot pedal. The stone wheel would whiz round whilst he did the sharpening.

I remember a young man being taken to a hut every day, where the Bowling Green is now, because it was believed then that the fresh air would ease his tuberculosis.

'AT NIGHT THE TRAMPS COULD BE SEEN CONVERGING ON MARKET BOSWORTH MAKING FOR THE WORKHOUSE'

There were several interesting characters in Market Bosworth. One, I remember, was a William Holmes, nicknamed Cocky, who was born in the Workhouse. As soon as he was able he was employed by various people. For many years he was employed by Grandma Rose Trivett and then by my mother and then by my uncle, Harry Trivett, at the Red Lion. He lived and slept in a small saddle room in the Red Lion yard for many years, almost until he died. He ended his days at the Workhouse in Station Road and at night the tramps could be seen converging on Market Bosworth making for the Workhouse. The other nearest workhouses were at Ashby and Nuneaton. In the morning they would start off again for one of these workhouses. There was another very small man, who was named Julian, who seemed to live by travelling between towns for work. I remember that there was also the rag-and-bone-man who gave children balloons in exchange for rabbit skins.

Laura Croman – The only time I ever got told off at school was by the Headmaster, Mr Graver. I was late back from lunch once, and that was because the houses in Sutton Lane were on fire; little did I know I would eventually be living there. The houses had thatched roofs and someone said that as the roads were being tarred and stoned, the tar-pot pipe, which acted as a chimney, had sent out sparks and the thatch had been set alight. When I lived in Sutton Lane, in later years, near to Mr Graver, he would take great delight in telling me that he had ordered his wife to close every window and door because of the fleas jumping out of the thatch!

Robert Jarvis – I remember the Quincentenary celebrations for the Battle of Bosworth when, after applying for permission from the health people, all the staff at Lampard's Butchers wore serf's clothes which consisted of a brown cloth tunic tied around the middle with a cord, a big floppy hat and pointed shoes. It went down very well, actually, in the village and I think everyone thoroughly enjoyed themselves. A Medieval Banquet was held in the Parish Field at the end of the week which was a very successful night.

Above: Workhouse, Station Road
Centre: Quincentenary shield in the Market Place

'JIM WAS A BIT LIKE FORD, THEY COULD DO A CAR IN ANY COLOUR AS LONG AS IT WAS BLACK. JIM COULD DO ANY HAIRCUT, AS LONG AS IT WAS SHORT-BACK-AND-SIDES'

One evening, an old fellow called Mr Poole was coming home from the pub and he noticed something unusual in the Market Place. He went home and fetched a pole and prodded the depression in the cobbles which collapsed, leaving a hole about five feet across and about thirty feet deep! It took quite a few loads of hard core to fill it in. No explorations were ever done that I can remember. It was thought that there could be tunnels to Bosworth Hall and different things like that, but as far as I know nothing was looked into. It was just filled up and concreted over.

Peter Loseby – Jim Kelly was the village barber. He worked in the house which is now the dental practice. Jim was about five foot eight I guess, glasses, an ever ready smile and black curly hair, well Brylcreamed. He had two chairs, one that was a swivel chair for the children and a nice straight-backed armchair for the men. You knew you had grown up when he stopped putting you on the swivel chair and put you in the armchair. It was a high point in your life. Jim was a bit like Ford, they could do a car in any colour as long as it was black and Jim could do any haircut as long as it was short-back-and-sides. He would not be pushed so when you knew you needed a haircut, you allocated a fair number of hours, unless you were there very early and got in first. Jim was a horse man, a betting man, so every so often he would just leave you in mid-haircut and disappear into another room and either put bets on or get some results for somebody and he would pass the time of day as you sat there. He was a smashing guy. I think it used to be a shilling for the boys and one and sixpence for the men and the only other thing that I like to recall of Jim, other than his smile, was when he would quietly ask, 'Anything for the weekend?' He would then go to a drawer in a glass-faced cupboard and fetch something out and hand it to the guy. Everybody else cast their eyes to the ground while this was taking place!

Brian Oakley – The only thing I can remember about Jim, is that he took a long time to cut your hair because he spent a lot of time looking up Station Road. He would do a few cuts and glance out of the bay window which looked straight up Station Road. He would do this a few times which, if you were in a bit of a rush, would get you a little bit worked up but you couldn't say anything.

The Square, Market Bosworth

'THE CHURN CAME FLYING OFF THE CART BUT CHARLIE DIDN'T GIVE A TOSS. HE KEPT ON GOING HELL FOR LEATHER!'

Peter Loseby – Jim also had a cut-throat razor; the strop for sharpening it hung beside the basin in front of him. I remember seeing Mr Stenton having his hair singed. Jim would light a taper and then run it up the back of Mr Stenton's neck, to cauterize the hair I suppose, I'm not sure what it was all about but it was only Bob Stenton who had that done.

There was also a Percy Quincey. Percy didn't work but he was the guy who used to sit alongside the organ in church and pump the bellows. When electricity was installed, there was no need for him to be there but as a tradition, he was always sitting there by the side of the organ.

'THE STANTONS WERE QUITE PROUD OF THE FACT THAT THEY HAD A TT HERD'

He did all the services Sunday morning and evening and lived with his sister, Ethel, in the house next to the Black Horse Inn which is now part of the restaurant. I always remember Percy for his big black boots, the way he walked with his eyes cast to the ground and the permanent grin on his face.

Sheila Loseby – Herbert Wright who lived in Park Street, opposite St Peter's Hall with his wife, was the caretaker at the Hall. He ruled the roost and was very strict. What he said went! When it came to a dance or other event on a Saturday night and it was supposed to finish at quarter to twelve, Herbert would walk across, open the doors and say, 'Time ladies and gentlemen please', as he switched off the lights.

Peter Loseby – Charlie Stanton lived with his brothers, Walter, Owen and Bill, opposite the Red Lion, and they farmed land off Station Road, near the railway line. Charlie was a character within the village because he delivered the milk from the back of a horse and cart. He had hand-held ladles which measured a pint or two pints into the housewife's jug and this was then stored in a bucket of cold water or on a thrawl. Charlie was a jockey and he did a bit of point-to-point racing. He did like his drink and he used to collect the money on a Saturday. The Stantons were quite proud of the fact that they had a TT herd (tuberculosis tested) and this was a good selling point for their milk. Charlie used to collect the money on a Saturday. One Saturday he had obviously been in the Red Lion and had a belly full of ale because he went down Station Road laughing his head off, horse at the gallop and the churn came flying off the cart but Charlie didn't give a toss. He kept on going hell for leather! People talked about it for months.

George Armson lived on Park Street by the entrance to the Dixie Arms. There were two cottages, now demolished; one on either side of what is now the car park. He was a carpenter and also the undertaker and the grave digger, along with Percy Poole.

'HE SHOVED THE TWO LADS OUT OF THE WAY AND TOOK THE ROCK HIMSELF WHICH BROKE HIS BACK'

He also provided the bier and I am pretty sure it was Mrs Armson who used to do the laying out. As a child, walking up to the junior school, you would very often see a coffin leaning up against the

workshop wall and as a little kid, it used to put the fear of God into you. George used to have a long tailed black coat and, with Fred Proudman the Verger, would push the coffin through the village up to the church. Fred had a top hat that was a couple of sizes too big, but it was not big enough to slip over his ears to blind him, so it used to rest nicely on his ears. The other thing about Fred Proudman was that as Verger, one of his duties at Holy Communion was to count how many people were in the congregation and count out the number of wafers required. He must have heard of stage whispers at some time because his voice resonated through the church as he whispered, in a very loud voice, TWENTY FIVE! He was always the last one to come for Communion and as he got hold of the Chalice he drained the remaining contents. He used to lean back at an angle with the Chalice up and clear it all out, he was a great guy and was a bit deaf as well.

Sid Moore was very big and his chest ran into his stomach. His claim to fame was that he was a Regimental Sergeant Major in the army, an RSM. Every Remembrance Sunday he would organise and lead the parade. The traffic stopped at 11 AM and he called the parade to, 'Attention!' His voice resonated around the Square when he dismissed the assembled crowd.

Jimmy Lively lived in a Nissen hut on Godsons Hill; eventually moving to The Crescent with his wife Joan and their children. Jimmy had accident after accident down the pit. He used to teach the new people down the pit and once there was a roof fall. He shoved the two lads he was training out of the way and took the rock himself which broke his back. It never got him down, he grumbled a lot but he got back onto his feet but he needed sticks. He was a hell of a character. The church was packed to standing when he died. He used to go on holiday on The Broads with Norman and Horace Cheshire, with Lol Glyde and Harold Hodges, and they used to go fishing. Jimmy went as the cook and on their return the regulars would gather in the King Bill to hear of their escapades on the trip. The Cheshires were skilled craftsmen, a carpenter, an electrician and a brickie. They were also part of a cracking darts team.

Top right: Armson's cottage, Park Street
Left: Dart's team, King Bill

'MRS CLARKE USED TO SIT ON A DESK TOP WITH HER FEET ON THE BENCH AND SHE WOULD SIT THERE LEGS AKIMBO'

Harry Frost, Headmaster of the St Peter's Primary School, used to go on holiday and whilst away would write the annual play for the school productions like the Petrified Gypsy and Cedric the Seahorse. Mrs Sabine was the reception class teacher in St Anne's Lodge. The next class was Mrs Fisher's. She used to shout in a very loud voice and stamp her foot on a regular basis.

Mr Heathcote and Mrs Clarke taught the oldest children. She was also a smoker of 'Craven A'. Her hair was grey and brushed back into a bun or plaits. Her husband farmed Glebe Farm in Station Road. She used to smoke like a trooper, bless her, and she was also the music teacher. One of the things that I remember about Mrs Clarke, and remember, I am a little kid so I would be ten or eleven, she used to read a piece of story from an Enid Blyton book or a similar book that kids used to bring in and she would read a chapter. On many a night Mr Frost would come in and say, 'I'm sorry you have got to stop because the buses are waiting'. Mrs Clarke used to sit on a desk top with her feet on the bench because the desk was integral with the bench, and she would sit there, legs akimbo. As children listening to the story, our eye line was some six inches off the desk top, and we were totally enthralled in what was going to happen to the Famous Five. As we looked we were treated to a sight - bloomers with elastic round the bottom. I always remember that she was very colour conscious because her underslip very often matched the colour of her bloomers. She was a lovely lady and it is a memory that will live with me forever. When you were that young it didn't have any connotation and Enid Blyton was more interesting anyway.

The Perrys were a family who farmed at South Farm on Shenton Lane. I only remember the mother and the two sons, Tertius and Sam. They were reputed to be the richest family in the village. They used to go to church every Sunday evening; the service started at 6.30 PM and they would come in at approximately twenty five minutes past six and walk across the width of the church by the font and sit halfway up.

Above: School play, The Petrified Gypsy
Right: South Farm

'IF YOU COULDN'T SPEAK GREEK OR LATIN THEN THERE WAS LITTLE HOPE FOR YOU'

The thing that should be remembered is that Sam was the eldest. Sam went into church in a brown suit, followed by his mother who wore a blue coat with a fox fur around her neck and a hat that came from the 1920s, a bonnet that pulled down, and Tertius wore a blue suit and he followed on behind. They looked neither left nor right, nor spoke to anyone as they walked through the church and sat in their pew looking at a brick wall which had got a monument to the Dixies in front of it. When Rector Pilling came, he asked me who these people were and I told him and I said, they are reputed to be the richest people in the village. 'Are they?' said Teddy. A little later on, it appears that Rector Pilling had gone down to the Perry's and suggested to them instead of looking at a blank wall, it would be much nicer if they had a stained glass window in front of them and a bit of an altar dedicated to the Dixie Grammar School. That is how that window on the left-hand side came to be there. People were aghast at how Rector Pilling, who hadn't been around too long, could elicit such funding. They always put a ten shilling note in the offertory plate; it was a lot of money then.

Now, I have a confession to make, I am sure I was not alone, but Mr Bark who kept the King William used to keep his cases of empty bottles outside in his backyard. The entrance to the outdoor off-licence used to be in the backyard. You used to get tuppence on empties and it has been known for certain members of the village to go round the back, pick two empty bottles out of the case that was piled there, go in the door that was the off-licence, and present the two empty bottles to Mr Bark who gave you four pence. Then you could go round to Lizzie Perry's *(where the Batter of Bosworth is now)* and give her the four pence for your gob-stoppers or your stick of liquorice.

Mr Gosling was the Headmaster at the Grammar School; a bachelor who ruled by fear. Mr Gosling was very learned in Greek and Latin and had written books on the languages. He judged people upon his own abilities and if you couldn't speak Greek or Latin then there was little hope for you. He lived on Harcourt Spinney with his house-keeper, Nelly, Nelly Mills.  Nelly had a box of rouge and used to put rouge on her cheeks so she always had a permanent flush. Mr Gosling loved his rugger and gave vociferous support from the touch line. People who were in fear of him still come back to the school reunion.

'WE USED TO PICK THE DOG-ENDS UP OUT OF THE GUTTER FOR HIM'

There are two hundred people who still come, fifty and sixty years afterwards, and talk of Mr Gosling with some affection and even I recognize that some of the discipline that he instilled in us didn't do us any harm at all. Academically the school was excellent, it really was excellent. He hated the fair that used to appear in the Square because that was a distraction. He had National Health glasses which he used to put on his forehead; his hair was plastered to his head, his parting down the middle. I don't know how he did it. I never did see him having his hair cut at Jim Kelly's!

Tramp Neddy was a homeless person who wandered the streets in a hat and an overcoat that was held together with binder twine. He needed a shave and his face was wrinkled with time but he wasn't a fearsome fella, he never bothered anyone. I know he used to do work down at Jackson's Farm in the Deepings and sleep in their barns and I think they kept an eye on him. I know every so often he was roped in by the authorities and taken down to the Workhouse and given a bath by Owen Stanton and a change of clothes, but he was not comfortable there. He was given a pair of new boots to get him going and off he'd trot on his wanderings again. He did eventually finish up at the Workhouse when he got too old. He used to sit on the bench outside the Workhouse with a permanent roll-your-own cigarette which was that thin, it could only have had about a strand of tobacco in it and it used to sit there in his mouth.

Another character was Joe Bright; Joe was a little man. He always reminded me of Charlie Chaplin with his little walking stick and the way he swaggered along, that Chaplin walk, then Joe Bright had a similar walk. He always wore a three piece suit, he had a moustache and I think he had curly hair. One of the things that Joe used to be very grateful to us kids for was that we used to pick the dog-ends up out of the gutter for him, and he used to then break open what was left of the cigarette, so that he could make his own. I always remember him because he had a pocket watch and a fairly big chain hanging across his waistcoat. He also had a medal and I never knew what that medal was. As kids, we obviously thought he had been a brave person in the war but I don't think it was a war medal. Joe was an avid supporter of the Hinckley Robins and I remember he was in the Hinckley Times, at one stage, when it was recognized that he used to walk from Bosworth to Hinckley.

Paul Oakley writes: I can remember one severe winter when six of us Carlton lads decided the ice on the canal was thick enough to take the weight of a car. So Philip Hunt, Bruce Milnthorpe, Harry Burnham, Howard Cockerill, Clive Middleton and myself, along with Edwin Milnthorpe on his motor bike, proceeded to drive the car, a Wolseley 10, belonging to Bruce, through the field on the left by Carlton Bridge and onto the canal. We took it in turns to drive the car towards Bosworth with a rope attached to it so we could pull Philip along on a cushion. Of course as we rounded a bend Philip swung out, hit the canal bank and bounced back, but he survived! As we approached Bosworth the ice got thinner because of the hot water that was being discharged from Timber Fireproofing Company so we quickly turned the car round and started back towards Carlton with great speed.

Thankfully we all managed to escape!

'THE BBC RADIO HAD THE TEMERITY OF CLAIMING TO HAVE FOUND CHICHESTER, WHICH THE ADMIRALTY WERE LESS THAN PLEASED WITH'

Peter Loseby – I was in the Navy serving on a boat called HMS Protector which was an ice patrol vessel down in the Antarctic. It was in 1968 and a man called Francis Chichester, a bit of a yachtsman, decided that in Gypsy Moth V, he would sail around the world single handed. It came to the time for him to approach Cape Horn and the media started building up that this guy. Nobody could survive the storms around Cape Horn and he would drown and disappear. It was decided by the Admiralty that we would go down to Cape Horn and patrol up and down off the Cape Horn until Gypsy Moth V with Chichester came by. I, at that stage, was the most experienced radar person, let's put it that way. So I was told to get on the radar and look for this contact which would be Chichester coming round. About 5 AM I picked up the contact on the radar, it was a firm contact at about eighteen, nineteen miles. I told the officer of the Watch that I believed I had got the contact and because the ship was incapable of taking the whole world's Press, all we had got on board was a representative of Reuters and a representative of United Press.

It was a foggy morning and at about 6 AM we blasted on the horn and there was this little boat with just a small sheet for a sail. Chichester, in his book said that he woke up as he approached Cape Horn (because he knew exactly where he was) to the noise of this siren and of all the places in the world where he thought he could have a few moments to

himself, it would have been there and he was not overly grateful.

Later I was rudely shaken at about 10.00 AM and went to the chart house and was told that the reporters wanted to have a quick word about what I did and how I discovered him. They also asked where I lived and I said I came from Market Bosworth in Leicestershire, job done!

'IT WAS IN 1968 AND A MAN CALLED

FRANCIS CHICHESTER, A BIT OF A

YACHTSMAN'

A little bit later that day I was woken again because there was a plane that had flown out from Punta Arenas. Little did we know that on that plane there was a Radio Newsreel reporter and a photographer from the Daily Express. They got an exclusive photograph of Chichester that nobody else had got, which broke all the agreements between Reuters, UPI and everybody else. The BBC Radio had the temerity of claiming to have found Chichester, which the Admiralty were less than pleased with. The BBC had to apologise to us. All of this was going on unbeknown to us and we just went about our business. Chichester turned left and started going up the Atlantic to come back home and we carried on doing our patrol.

'MOTHER EXPLAINED THAT HER SON HAD ALWAYS WANTED TO BE AN ADMIRAL'

It appears that the Leicester Mercury said, 'We have got a local hero here'. Out to Bosworth they went, found mother scrubbing the back door step, said to mother, 'Have you got a son called Peter who's in the Antarctic?' and mother said, 'Yes', thinking that the boat had sunk or I had died or something. They said, 'He has found Chichester and he's quite famous now.' Mother thought that she would be helpful if she explained that her son had always wanted to be an Admiral. This was not good news, good news for the rest of the world to hear that this guy had got aspirations, but to be ribbed relentlessly from then on, even to today where Mr Heathcote calls me Admiral - How is the Admiral now?

Winifred Smith writes: I remember my Grandma Lewis telling me of her memories of moving to Market Bosworth with the Timber Fireproofing Company in 1920. The men relocated from Fulham, London, to work here with the Company. The men either lodged at the Dixie Arms Hotel or Hollier's farmhouse, now Moorland House in Barton Road, until the wooden bungalows were built for them on Station Road. Their families then joined them towards the end of 1921. What a change for those families coming to Market Bosworth in 1921 from the streets of terraced houses in Fulham, to a country road with fields all around and almost a mile from shops, school and church. The first house on the way to the Square was the thatched cottage, now known as Aylesbrook Cottage.

My grandmother used to go on the train to Nuneaton. The station provided employment for many over the years. The passenger trains stopped in the1930s. My mother, Win Lewis, married Ted Pratt who came from South Wigston to work as a signal man at Bosworth Station. When married, my parents lived in one of the new council houses on Station Road, known as The Crescent, in December 1932 and my mother lived there until her death in 1990.

Olive Hicklin – I'd be about thirteen and a half when my mum had Pam. She was only at the Park Infirmary for two days and she caught a fever so she had to go to Markfield Sanatorium and she stayed there until she got better. When my dad went to visit the newborn baby, the Sister said to him, 'This is a hospital for sick people and there is nothing wrong with this baby', so he brought her home. Madge and I took it in turns to look after her. I didn't go to school and the school bobby, Mr Grey, used to come every Monday for weeks and weeks and he would always make me jump because I would be in the wash-house over the dolly-tub with the baby in the pram in the yard. He would say, 'How is your mother?' and I would say, she is going on alright. 'And when do you think she will be coming home?' To which I replied, I didn't know. He asked as to when I would be going back to school. I never did go back. That was it. I was leaving at Christmas anyway.

'IF YOU WERE DRUNK THE PONY WOULD TAKE YOU HOME'

Martin Shepherd – I was quite young when I lived at Market Bosworth and we used to bring our horses up to the forge to be shod there, when Clem Phillips used to be blacksmith. If he was shoeing a horse at about 1 PM, his wife would shout him for dinner and she would perhaps shout about three times. While he was doing a job he wouldn't go for his dinner. He was a tough man who could do anything with iron. He used to go to the shows as well. He was quite a character. Often we would pick our stuff that he had repaired when we came to the dances at St Peter's Hall and put them in the car before we went into the dance. He would still be there working. I don't think his wife saw a lot of him. He was a great chap really.

Old Bill Lampard was a character; he used to play the violin in the Black Horse at Christmas time. Grandma would say, bring your violin up, Bill, and he would sit there and play it; a beautiful violinist, was Mr Lampard.

The Longs were related to my grandma; Mrs Long was my grandma's sister. They used to have a shop where the Bank is now. Mr Insley, the butcher, was there when I was in Bosworth. He had a half door which he would lean over. It was opposite my grandma's at the Black Horse and you would go by

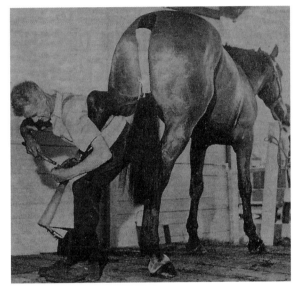

and get up to different things, as young kids do. He used to say, 'I'm watching you my lad, I shall tell your grandma'. We didn't like him much at that time. The Longs had their slaughterhouse down at the end of Back Lane, on the corner with the footpath. The slaughterhouse doors and the garage doors used to be our goal posts. Uncle Bob Long used to come out and say, 'I've had enough of you lot!' because every time the ball hit the back of the net it hit the doors. The thing I remember, because I used to go to that school down there, was the pigs squealing when they were killing them. My father told us he used to go from the bottom end of Carlton to the pub in the pony and trap and would tie it up. Coming back he would put two lights on and if he was drunk the pony would take him home.

Angela Hutton – I remember going up to St Peter's Hall to get our Coronation mugs, I can remember that quite vividly. They also had a cinema there; I tend to think it was on a Tuesday, I remember seeing Bambi there. I also remember the Vero's up the park; they used to have garden fêtes, where the Country Park is now. We used to go on the lake on a boat.

Clem Phillips, the blacksmith

CONGERSTONE PRIMARY SCHOOL

AFTER INITIAL DISCUSSION WITH CLASS TEACHER, MRS LIS JACKSON, THE
CHILDREN OF CONGERSTONE PRIMARY SCHOOL WERE INTERVIEWED BY
JUDIE CLARK, TEACHING ASSISTANT, TO GIVE THEIR PERCEPTION OF SCHOOL LIFE
AS YEAR 4 PUPILS:

Contributors to this section were the pupils of Year 4, Congerstone Primary School and class
teacher, Mrs Lis Jackson with help from teaching assistant, Judie Clark.

I walk to school from my grandma's usually and I leave there at twenty five to nine. It's very
helpful that the school is in Congerstone. On my way to school, I meet up with my friend…when I
get to the War Memorial. There is quite a lot of people walk to school, there is a lot of people to talk
to and meet, so you can always have a chat. I find it more freedom than if you were with a grown
up.

Before morning lessons begin, we have to read for about five or ten minutes, depending on what
time you get in. The doors open at about twenty to nine and then they close at about five to and then
we all sit and read as soon as we arrive. Then at about five to nine we have to have something called
Registration and it's to see if everyone is there or not at five to nine, between five to nine and nine
o'clock, we have to go into Assembly.

Then after that we have to go into lessons.

During the week our lessons include: Maths, Literacy, Science, ICT, Swimming, Art, DT, which is
Design and Technology, PE, Physical Education, Geography, History, French, PSHE (*Personal
Social and Health Education*) and Religious Education.

At playtime children are allowed, healthy stuff, which can be a yoghurt or fruit or vegetables and
then we have a drink as well, like water or milk, something that you bring from home; or school do
milk and juices, which you have to pay for.

We have a few more lessons followed by lunch; we can either have hot dinner or bring your own
packed lunch. But we are not allowed fizzy drinks.

We play out on the playground or on the field, if it's really warm and the field is dry. After lunch
we do another lesson.'

My favourite thing that I do at lunchtime is 'Huff and Puff'. It's like lots of different equipment that
you can play with. My favourite thing is probably the balancing board. Well, you put your feet at
either end then you can rock side to side.

One of my favourite lessons is Literacy because, at the moment, we are doing Kensuke's Kingdom
and Mrs Jackson is reading out to us and we are writing our own story based on the story.

I like doing group reading because we do plays and Mrs Watson is doing a group and I have not
been in it yet and I can't wait.

'WE DID THIS VOLCANO OUT OF VINEGAR AND BI-CARBONATE OF SODA'

I really like Literacy also, because we do poems and write stories.

Well I like doing Art because it's very fun and I like drawing and I'm quite good at painting. I liked doing the Aboriginal art because I like the way they do just little blobs and lines, like they fit it all in.

I like doing dance because, at the moment, we are doing global warming and in the past we have done dancing which reflects global warming.

I think Science is amazing because we are always doing exciting and amazing experiments. We did this volcano out of vinegar and bi-carbonate of soda.

Well, I enjoy the trips, they are quite exciting and it's lovely to have a day out, not stuck in the classroom, have a bit of fresh air and have a look around, see some other places.

We once did the Tudors and we went to Bosworth Battlefield. That was brilliant because there was a man that showed us that there was all kinds of things that they used when there was war. We went to Donnington le Heath Manor House and we did different things like setting the table.'

To stay active, there is a range of activities and clubs to choose from, football club, swimming, tag rugby, running, golf, judo, fencing, aerobics, youth games, gymnastics and athletics.

The reason we do quite a lot of clubs is because they are fun and entertaining because otherwise you could be sick bored watching telly.

We are really lucky to have all of this sport at our school, Congerstone. It's a great opportunity to get yourself fit and healthy and make yourself to live a bit longer.

We are really lucky to have Mr Fitt, our sports teacher, as well, because he makes it more fun and easy but not too easy for the bigger ones. He makes it fun and understandable.

As well as having a willow classroom and gardens, the environment is utilised as a resource for learning. Our school is an Eco-school because we do lots of things to help the environment. We have a bird hide, a pond, gardens and we also do Eco-days, which is where schools that don't have as good an environment as we have and aren't as lucky, get to come over to our school and do fun environmental based activities.

When it's a nice day, the younger classes will occasionally go out and do pond dipping. They will look at the creatures under a microscope and then let them go back to their natural habitat.

At school we have three gardens: The Sunshine Garden, the Sensory Garden and the Gardening Club garden.

'I WOULDN'T LIKE TO BE ANYWHERE ELSE IN THE WORLD'

The Willow Classroom is a classroom made out of willow and it is in the shape of a dome. People go in there when it is really hot and cool down and talk quietly with their friends.

Fund raising events are also part of school life; The Friends are people that organise different things… summer fairs, everything like that, they do. It's for us and it's really, really good.

We have a charity in Sri Lanka, to help re-build a school, (*after the Tsunami*), and we also fund a hospital as well, so all the money we raise from, like, other things, goes to the zoo, the hospital or to Sri Lanka.

We have a special school, but I think about all the people that haven't got such cool stuff as what we've got. That's why we raise things for them.

We are very lucky to have a school like ours and I'm so happy that I come to this school because I wouldn't like to be anywhere else in the world.

Lis Jackson, class teacher – I have been teaching at Congerstone Primary School for over ten years. The school has a very rural setting in Congerstone; it was originally part of the Gopsall Estate. We are going up to 140 pupils at the moment.

I teach English, we call it Literacy now. I teach History and RE so I am always trying to find links between all of those, and support that with art education, dance and music as well.

The school is a very sporty school, most of our children do over five hours of sport a week and that's either sports that they do as part of their lessons in the curriculum, or there is a very wide programme of pre-school and after school sports events.

I like the community feel of the school, I like the family atmosphere that we have. It is quite an exciting place to work, every day is different really. We have a very strong parent-teacher body, very strong Governors as well, which kind of lead us and support us in everything we want to do. Our school is an Eco-school and a healthy-living school, so the eco-nature of the school is that the children are very aware of sustainability and recycling.

We welcome students, we welcome people that are being trained to be teachers, we welcome young people that want to come in and do work experience. We do end up with positive, motivated, happy young people who are ready to face the world when they leave.

Left: Willow classroom
Far left: Congerstone Primary School